THE
JOURNEY®

CONSCIOUSNESS
THE NEW CURRENCY

May our lives be lived as a never ending
prayer of gratitude to the infinite grace
that pervades all of life

"As people see their predicament clearly –
that our fates are inextricably tied together, that life is a mutually
interdependent web of relations – then universal responsibility becomes
the only sane choice for thinking people."

~ Dalai Lama

THE JOURNEY®

CONSCIOUSNESS
THE NEW CURRENCY

A New Paradigm for Manifesting Conscious Abundance,
Lasting Fulfilment and a Sustainable Future

BRANDON BAYS

—— AND ——

KEVIN BILLETT

Copyright © 2009 by Brandon Bays and Kevin Billett

First published in the United Kingdom in 2009 by Journey Publications Ltd.
A division of The Journey®

The rights of Brandon Bays and Kevin Billett to be identified as the authors of the work has been asserted by them in accordance with the Copyright, Designs and Patents Act 1988.

A CIP catalogue record for this title is available from the British Library.

ISBN 978-0-9563379-0-0

Authors' photograph by Mark James Billett

Typeset in Optima by York Publishing Services.
Printed and bound by Gomer Press, Llandysul, Ceredigion SA44 4JL

Journey Publications Ltd
PO Box 2, Cowbridge, CF71 7WN, United Kingdom

INTRODUCTION

If humanity is to survive, it will be due to a global shift in consciousness. This book is a celebration of and a manual for that shift. It is a practical guide that can awaken you to your true potential, allowing you to live gracefully, wholesomely, joyously in abundance even in this challenging era of global uncertainty.

Deep inside us all is a huge radiant potential, a power of life that can create miracles, a creative genius that can answer our deepest questions and inspire solutions to our most pressing difficulties, a love that is capable of healing all things, a peace that defies all boundaries of separation. When we are born it is as if life gives each of us an invisible passport inscribed with the words, *"You are brilliant, gifted, full of grace. You are here to be part of the astonishing co-creative dance of manifestation. You deserve to live freely, fully, consciously in abundance, and you are invited to serve and nourish life, as part of life. You have so much to offer, you are more than qualified for the job, and life is hiring".*

Yet within a short while we seem to lose touch with our invisible passports. We forget the invitation life made and can't recall how to access the vast expanse of our potential. In time the largeness of our being recedes into the background and we end up denying the extraordinary genius that is our own innate nature as we contract in our beings. Ultimately we end up encased in a mould that feels small, limited, even shut down.

We are being rocked by some of the biggest wake up calls in history. Our planet is in a state of crisis on so many levels: environmentally, financially, politically and socially. We are living in a time of turmoil, of huge systemic challenge. Humanity's true greatness is being called upon like never before: life *needs* our inspired creativity, our intelligent solutions, our selfless, love-driven actions. Our continued existence depends on it.

But in our forgetting we become immobilised by fear-consciousness, and we react to every new crisis or challenge by shutting down, getting lost in uncertainties or denial. We put a lid over ourselves and our world becomes smaller. We disempower ourselves. Less of our innate greatness is available and we can no longer access the inherent creative genius and inspired action that in openness and health is available to us all. Our consciousness adds to the fear-consciousness currently gripping our world and *we* become part of the problem, instead of part of the solution.

Yet despite our unhealthy conditioned responses to the demands of life, a deeper part of us knows there is a different way forward, a greater possibility. Somewhere inside us is a knowing that living authentically, purposefully in wholesome abundance is a destiny we deserve and can embrace. This destiny is calling us. It is a quiet and compelling pull that is drawing us into a fresh, new expansiveness, and it cannot be ignored.

That fact that you chose this book and are reading these words is a sign, a confirmation that you are responding to this call. Some deep level of your being recognises this. Something is pulling you to investigate and experience this greater authentic possibility.

Your essence is an expansive potential that is completely free, already whole. It is beckoning you to open beyond your fears and conditioning; it is inviting you to break free from the negative paradigms of our times. It is begging you to shed the shackles of fear-consciousness that diminish and immobilise you. It is calling you into an infinite field of all possibilities where access to inspired answers and creative solutions are effortlessly available – even when life seems to insist that such answers and solutions do not exist.

This infinite field longs to embrace you, to use you as a vehicle for a *new* type of abundance, one born directly from open, truthful awareness, one that effortlessly embraces *all* of life; an abundance that experiences the totality of life, each individual aspect and component, as an integral part of itself; an abundance that is a guardian of the health and wellbeing of *all* its parts, and acts for the greater good of the whole. An abundance that forgives, shares, heals and is a reflection of our deepest desires to live in a fully expressed love, and to be a contribution to the planet rather than a drain on its resources. This book gives us the ability to liberate ourselves and to begin living from this wholesome abundance-consciousness.

Old school, market-driven materialism, with its *me-first* myopia and its wanton excesses, is already archaic. As a system it is broken and defunct, and it has failed us colossally. Unconscious consumption has been the cause of a great rift in humanity. Its compulsive consumerism, its obsessive competitiveness, its selfish denials were all driven by fear – fear of lack, fear of threat, fear of failure, fear of loss of security. Thankfully, it is no longer hip nor cool, no longer the zeitgeist. As an ideal it is dead. And if humanity is to survive it is no longer an option.

We are now being invited to uncover and embrace a new model of abundance, one that is consciously aligned with the greater good, one that is inclusive – one born from gratitude, generosity and a cherishing of the blessing of life. It is time to move forward into a new era of abundance-consciousness; one that is accepting and encouraging, one that is deeply fulfilling and embraces all of life.

Our planet, our home, is demanding a greater largeness of being. It is demanding an entire shift in our awareness, in the way we think, in the way we act, in the way we *are*. Ultimately it is demanding a fundamental shift in consciousness itself. It will be seen in the ways we do business, in our intelligent use of planetary resources, in our understanding of the interdependence of all living systems, in our love of diversity, in our tolerance of differences, and in our generosity of heart. These will be the natural expressions of a more fundamental change in the way we know ourselves.

Consciousness *is the new currency.*

Consciousness is a powerful, compelling force for change. In every age there have been inspired individuals who went against the tide of conventional restrictive norms and beliefs, people who single-pointedly stayed true, even in the face of extreme hardship, persecution or calamity. With such beings, the powerful transmission of their consciousness, their simple yet potent ability to stay wide open and immersed in a vaster, more inclusive awareness was such a radical catalyst for transformation that in many cases it altered the course of human history.

In the last century we have been blessed with very powerful examples. Mahatma Gandhi was uncompromising in his certainty that the power of compassion and nonviolence would free his country. Through the force of that consciousness alone, he became the primary catalyst for India's liberation from British rule. Gandhi was a living transmission of his own words, '*Be* the change you wish to see in the world'. Nelson Mandela, a conscious embodiment of compassion and forgiveness, accomplished the seemingly impossible when he galvanised the nonviolent end to apartheid in South Africa and became the country's first black president. He continues to be an inspiration to people the world over as an example of the power of one person's commitment to his ideals. Martin Luther King, Jr. was a man with a dream – a dream so compelling, a vision so powerful that it continues to shape the way we think to this day. He was a conscious embodiment of his message of liberty, and his vision of freedom and equality began a process that continues to erode the roots of prejudice and intolerance in America, indeed throughout the world.

What all these great souls share in common is that their individual expression of consciousness shaped history and reshaped humanity. Though the general consensus was that their dreams were impossible, through the power of consciousness alone they made the *im*possible possible. It was not what they *did*, but *who they were* that made the difference. They were not just part of the solution, their *consciousness <u>was</u> the solution*. The power of consciousness itself accomplished miracles.

And, of course, we are not talking about the greatness, the consciousness of just these specific exemplars. **All consciousness is already here. All the greatness that has *ever been*, is available in this moment. Their greatness is your greatness – it is the same greatness. It resides in you. It is your true essence. Their consciousness is your consciousness – it is the same consciousness. It is who you are.**

~

There is an imperative, a demand for a conscious transformation and it can no longer be denied. Every honest person knows it: **something <u>has</u> to change**.

We are at a time in our evolution when we can no longer simply rely on the conviction and strength of a few rare individuals. We can no longer passively rely on *anyone* else to make this shift for us – not a few elite geniuses, visionaries or saints, not our politicians, our religious leaders, nor our corporate magnates, and not future generations. Everything now relies on *us*. The time has come to access our potential greatness and to let this greatness use us to the fullest. The time has come to *decide* to be part of the wave of awakening and healing that is currently sweeping our planet, a shift in consciousness our world so desperately needs. For true change to come about, for *real* transformation to take place, *we must decide* that it will start with us, with you and with me. This is a demand for a change that can only take place from the inside out and this book was written in answer to this call.

It is time to wake up. Not as another fanciful distraction or casual experiment but as an absolute imperative. If our world is to heal, if humanity is to survive, if as a species and as individuals we are to thrive, we *must* find a new way of living, a new way of interacting and cooperating – not as a rehash of old ideas, concepts or beliefs; not merely with more rules or different governances – but by *stopping and opening*, by letting go of and healing from our unhealthy past, and by opening into our boundless potential and moving forward in a fresh, new consciousness.

It is time to stop. It is time to open beyond our excuses and our perceived limitations. It is time to be done with our fear-based values and doctrines. It is time to listen more acutely than ever before, time to tell a keener, deeper truth. It is time not just to break a paradigm, but to *break with the paradigm of the <u>known</u>*. It is time to open freshly into the expansiveness of the *unknown* and to discover its power to bring about miracles.

Some books and strategies tell us that the answer is to hold bigger visions and to get more ambitious in our goal setting. But what we are proposing is not simply about the power of positive thinking and repeating more positive affirmations. It is not about stirring up a more fiery personal conviction, nor drumming up a stronger personal will to overcome our circumstances. Nor is it about denying ourselves or becoming self-sacrificing martyrs, confirming some false sense of spiritual nobility. It is not about telling ourselves more stories *about* our fears. Nor is it about overriding or ignoring our fears; it is not about pushing them away, pretending they don't exist, or transcending them. It is not about reframing them into something more manageable. These are ego-based strategies that have brought us to where we are right now. They are short-term expedients that ultimately didn't work. They have *never* really worked.

The demand is a greater one. It is a demand for us to *get real*. The true demand is that we stop for long enough to uncover, face and *meet* our own deepest fears and insecurities, and to free ourselves from their grip, so that they no longer unconsciously drive our destructive behaviours. It is a call to uncover the silent saboteurs that have limited our lives and to finish with them once and for all. It is an imperative to open beyond all limitations into our deepest potential, which is whole, free and bursting with creative inspiration and solutions. This is a call for true liberation and a call to take conscious action born from this freedom.

In our heart each one of us wants these things; in our souls we crave them. We feel a light beckoning from deep inside, bidding us to remove the lampshade, to liberate an inherent magnificence that until now has remained hidden. We long to thrive and flourish as individuals. We long to be a proactive force for change, to act in concert with a higher purpose, to feel that there has been some tangible and lasting benefit to life from our short stay on this planet. We long to make a real difference for ourselves, our loved ones, and our communities. We yearn to live life consciously, recognising and utilising *all* of our true potential. Yet no one told us how.

This book was written to teach you how. It will give you the means to access the innate genius inside you and will enable you to begin living from that greatness. It offers simple, effective tools and powerful process work to clear out the limitations, negative constructs and emotional blocks that have put a lid over your life and made you play small. It will give you process work to expose and liberate silent saboteurs and will offer you ways to meet and clear out your old fears, so you can be a fuller, more vibrant and alive expression of your true self. This book will allow you to open into the infinite potential that is your soul and will give you the practical means to live an authentically guided life of freedom, fullness, and abundance.

This is an experiential book. The work is born from direct experience. Tens of thousands of people have already used the process work and discovered true freedom. They have liberated their own radiant, abundant potential. We have used and continue to regularly use this work on ourselves, to deeper and deeper effect. It is designed to carry you into a direct experience of your limitless potential. It is not a theory or a formula but an expression of living truth that has had profound and lasting results for people from all over the world.

With this book, you too will have the ability to open into inspired and creative solutions and catalyse healthy abundance in all areas of your life. If you use its work and live from the truth of your own potential, it will give you the results you have been seeking your whole life. And as you live in the fullness of your own potential you will become a living transmission of *possibility-consciousness*. Your very presence will awaken those around you, and you will become a force for conscious, positive change. Your actions will be a mirror of that inspiration and they will catalyse others to also take conscious action. And, as with the rare souls who have gone before, the ripples of your awakened consciousness will continue to reverberate over time.

This is your chance to become a living expression of conscious abundance that is and has always been your destiny.

CHAPTER 1

We are living in a time when nothing can be relied upon, nothing can be counted on, where nothing is genuinely secure. There is nowhere that we can go where we can be truly safe. Uncertainty is everywhere. No one is immune. No culture is excluded. No country is exempt.

Our planet is in peril of ecological breakdown. The world's population continues to burgeon and increase its demands on precious natural resources even at a time when our economies are the most damaged they have been in decades. Massive corporations and major financial institutions that we believed would be rock solid for generations to come have crumbled or have needed truly gigantic financial support. In recent times our homes have been repossessed, our jobs have been lost or become insecure and our pensions plans have collapsed in value. Even the USA, the most powerful economic and military force in the world, has been exposed as being as vulnerable to violent attack as almost any other country on the planet. Today, absolutely no one is immune to the effects of diseases and natural disasters that seem to become more widespread each year. Random, drug-related, and domestic violence is common. More marriages end in divorce than stand the test of time, and an ever-increasing number of children are brought up in unstable families or broken homes. Life as we once knew it is under threat. Indeed, every aspect of our personal lives – from our environment, our careers and financial security, to our physical security, our relationships, lifestyles and family lives – is in jeopardy.

But the truth is, it has *always* been this way. There has always been uncertainty. Throughout time there have always been wars, conflicts, famines, epidemic diseases and catastrophic natural disasters. There have always been periods of social upheaval and economic collapse. To live a human life is tenuous at best. There have never been any guarantees.

Yet like some mutually agreed mass hypnosis, for the last five or six decades many of us have played a superficial game of make-believe, and lived in the *illusion that we were safe*. We have existed in a bubble of false security; cocooned in an unreal, idealised pretence that life would always remain much as it was. We convinced ourselves that wars took place only in other countries, that human deprivations applied only to foreigners, that disasters took place only in other people's cities. We deluded ourselves that those threats 'out there' did not really apply to us. Catastrophes were what happened on the news, to *other* people. The crises shown on TV seemed removed from our daily existence. They did not touch *our* personal lives or the lives of *our* families.

We have all seen so many disaster movies that when genuine catastrophe struck it took on an unreal or even a surreal quality. We have become so accustomed to on-screen images of devastation that we have become inured to the real thing. For those of us living in Western-style societies, when the catastrophic tsunami of 2005 occurred in southeast Asia and hundreds of thousands of lives were lost, its power to shock and impact us was short lived, and our attention soon turned to more pressing, more current news.

Most of us have become desensitised, detached and disengaged from the pain of reality. Until recently our collective heads have been firmly planted in the sand, and we have lived in denial. We have lived in the delusion of security. Security does not exist, has *never* existed.

But in recent years our world has been giving us an earth-shattering wake up call that will not be ignored. The world is demanding that we shed the comfortable false cocoons we have built around our lives and wake up to the truth of what is actually happening. It is shaking us out of our taciturn, blinkered existence and is shoving reality into our face.

Disasters that once upon a time were happening somewhere outside our spheres of existence, to people we had no real connection to, are coming perilously close to our own lives. In many cases they are directly affecting us, or are impacting the lives of those we love in a very real way. These crises are no longer happening 'out there', they are taking place right here, right now. They have become personal.

Life is doing everything it can to shake us out of our complacency, and penetrate our patterns of sleepiness and denial. It is requiring of us a new, more honest, more authentic way of being. But unfortunately, because we have lived for so many years in the fantasy realm of denial-consciousness, when real life confronts us and threatens our personal lives, nearly all of us freeze in response. We are so unprepared to have our bubble burst that when it does we get mired in fear.

None of us were given the manual, *How to Healthily Respond to Unexpected Crisis*, so it is natural that our first instinctive response is to freeze. We automatically put up barricades and scramble into our minds, into something known, seeking in vain to find safety. We try to deny what is happening, we withdraw from it, or we fly into desperate, futile activity as a way of avoiding it, and our awareness shuts down, our being shuts down and our ability to access creative, empowering responses recedes and becomes unavailable to us.

Ultimately, we get paralysed in fear, numbness, non-action and blame. We become incapable of positive pro-action. Our world inevitably becomes smaller and smaller. Our ability to embrace creative solutions diminishes until we end up stymied, lost, ineffectual. Instead of being part of the solution we *become* the problem. Our collapsed, defeated consciousness only adds to our inability to act. It kills our ability to access innovative solutions and inspired answers.

~

At a recent Manifest Abundance retreat, I found out just how destructive and pervasive this fear-consciousness can be. On the first night we were exploring how each of us has *hidden comfort zones* in every area of our life. How we live life only to a certain contained level, in a false sense of security buffered by a comfortable envelope beyond which we dare not venture. How we rarely, if ever, challenge ourselves to stretch beyond that cushy, soothing blanket of the *known*.

We were exploring what it would feel like to step outside these comfort zones, what it would feel like to stretch beyond our world of the *known*. I thought it would be pertinent to bring our current world consciousness of financial crisis into the room, to make things more real, as many of us have not directly experienced a huge catastrophe or crisis in our lives, and genuinely do not know how we would respond. So I invited everyone to make the exercise as personally real and authentic as possible.

I instructed them, "Imagine you are in an era of financial turmoil and uncertainty, and that you are working for a business that is experiencing acute financial difficulties serious enough to put people's jobs on the line. At work, all the employees are aware that for the company to survive radical changes need to take place, new ways of operating need to be found."

I asked everyone to really imagine that they were *in* this scenario. Then I invited them to experience what it would feel like to know that exciting, innovative and inspired ideas about how to streamline, expand and grow the business were arising in their awareness. I also cautioned them that with every new and untested idea there would be a risk. Their ideas might save the company, or they might just cause the company to go under and their co-workers to lose their jobs. With innovation there is always uncertainty. There can be no assurances of success, but the possibility exists that a new way of working might just be the thing to turn the business around and bring abundance into the lives of all concerned.

Then they were to imagine presenting these new ideas to their board of directors, and to feel what that was like. They were to note how they acted, what they thought, and how they responded emotionally; to fully experience what it was really like to offer their creative solutions to the board knowing there were no guarantees of success.

The participants really threw themselves in and played the game fully. After this elicitation I asked people to share their experiences. Some people said that they just could not present their ideas to the board because they were afraid of being exposed as fools and it was not worth the risk, or that they were so hesitant when they tried to put their ideas forward that they became ineffectual and no one listened. But a significant portion of participants in the room had quite a different response. Several successful business owners shared that they felt excited by the idea of offering radical, innovative ideas to another company, and that as they did not own the company, and the bottom line risk was not theirs, they had nothing to lose. They were fired up, inspired and excited about the fresh ideas and possibilities that were arising, and felt like they could be an important catalyst for positive change in someone else's firm. They did not even contemplate the possibility of failure, and they were sure their ideas were constructive and grounded ones, which might even bring the firm resounding success.

Next I asked everyone to imagine a slightly different scenario; that once again we were in an era of financial crisis, but that this time *their own* business was floundering, and they were aware that for it to survive innovative and radical changes would need to take place. Inspired ideas and creative solutions to streamline, realign and grow were needed if they were to keep their company afloat, and it would be up to them to come up with and implement these innovations. It would require them to invest in their own business, and yet the situation was the same. With innovation comes risk, and there are no guarantees. I asked them to really experience how this would make them feel and to share what their true internal response was.

What a shocking difference there was in their reactions to the second scenario. Several successful business owners spoke openly about how they froze at the thought of taking this risk, and that their fears about failing were so paralyzing that they could not come up with even one inspired solution or one constructive idea that could save their company. One woman shared that she gave up before she had even tried. She was so certain she would fail that she was defeated before she even attempted to find new answers. Another man said he panicked and then froze so completely that he could not even think.

He said, "I became so blocked and locked into my fear that I couldn't move in any direction. And, Brandon, this is *exactly* what is occurring right now in my life. The truth is, my successful business is currently floundering, my employees livelihoods are at stake, and though I could come up with thousands of creative solutions for *someone else's company*, when it comes to my own firm I'm stuck. I'm afraid that if I move in *any* new direction I will create catastrophe, and so I am immobilised, so stymied that I fear if I invest my own personal money in it I will be throwing good money after bad. Though I don't doubt my ability to turn *someone else's* company around – I absolutely *know* I have the talent and potential to do that – the possibility that I might fail in my *own company* is keeping me trapped and incapable of being pro-active at a time when it is imperative that I take effective action.

If I am honest, the truth is that at the deepest level I don't believe I have what it takes to survive in the face of real crisis. I'm so afraid that someone or something is going to lower the boom, and that if I don't break free from this trap, my company won't survive, my family won't survive – I won't survive."

In just a few short sentences this baldly honest man had accurately encapsulated exactly what is occurring in our world right now.

We all have been living in our day-to-day worlds, feeling relatively secure in the belief that everything will continue much as it has done in the past, and even if it has been a struggle or a battle, still it is a struggle we understand, a battle we *know*.

Yet with the big shake-ups our world is giving us, with the accelerating increase in world crises, there has been one blow after another and nothing seems secure anymore. And a fear that has long remained dormant inside us has been reawakened by the tumult. This fear is the oldest fear known to humankind. It is our most primordial, instinctive fear, a fear for our lives – a fear that we might not have the ability to survive in a crisis.

This fear is so powerful that we freeze and shut down when the faintest whisper of it arises from within. We have spent our whole lives sublimating it, protecting ourselves from it, hiding from it, and trying in vain to escape it. But unless we turn and face the tiger in the eye; unless we meet this fear head on, get to its very root and clear it out, it will continue to run our lives and clamp us down at the very time when we need to access our greatest potential. As long as we don't face and clear it, it owns us. It keeps a lid on our lives at the moment we most need to take the lid off! It paralyses us when we most need to open wide into our fullest potential and have access to infinite possibilities and inspired, newly creative solutions.

The good news is that there is real hope. With The Journey process work we have been offering for the last 15 years, we have discovered and developed powerful, effective ways to penetrate these blocks, break down these solid-seeming structures, expose the silent saboteurs and stuckness, and clear them out so completely that we are left wide open in a vast field of all possibilities – a field so free, so clear, so saturated with unborn potential, that answers and solutions are right here, immediately and effortlessly available to us. This greatness within you is not only accessible, it is your own essence, and everyone, and I mean everyone, is capable of getting to the roots of their own blocks and silent saboteurs, and clearing them completely. Everyone is capable of opening into the boundless presence of their own soul – where true genius, greatness, creativity, innovation, love, and freedom are all present and fully available.

I had the personal experience of the phenomenon of the incapacitating effect of fear some time ago, when the universe did lower the boom on my life for several years running. Through one disaster after another – the very types of crises that are affecting many of us right now – I had to finally meet and face my own fear for survival.

It all started in 1992 when, at age 39, at what seemed to be the prime of my life, I was diagnosed with a basketball-sized tumour. The severity of the diagnosis catapulted me into a profound and emotionally splaying spiritual journey, where I uncovered a means to so completely clear issues stored at a cellular level that my body healed naturally in only six and a half weeks.

But this tumour turned out to be just the beginning of a series of crises that came one upon the next. A year after the tumour had healed, there were catastrophic wildfires in Malibu, California that were so ferocious that hundreds of miles of land and wildlife were destroyed. It was declared a national disaster. 280 homes were burnt to the ground, and mine was one of them. The loss wiped us out financially.

A year later we were struggling to put our life back together, and had moved south of the burnt-out area. We had written to the IRS asking to be put on the tax deferment plan that had been offered to those devastated by the fires. Instead, the authorities contacted our employers and seized 100 per cent of both our salaries, and froze our bank accounts.

Three days later, my husband confessed that he had fallen in love with another woman, and over the next year our 20-year marriage was torn apart and dissolved. During that year my job, and hence my income, was cut back by my employer, and eventually it fell away completely.

At the age of 39 I had faced a life-threatening illness. At 40 my uninsured home and my personal possessions had been completely destroyed by fire. At 41 my income was confiscated, and my cherished marriage fell apart. And at 42 my employment wound down and ended. I was left alone having lost everything that mattered, everyone I cared about, even the profession and the lifestyle I had identified with, that I felt defined me.

The universe had taken my perfect, ideal life and had taught me that *nothing* was secure. I had trusted my youthful, vibrant, healthy body and it had betrayed me with a life-threatening illness. I had trusted in the warmth and safety of our beautiful seaside home, and it had burnt to the ground, leaving me homeless. I had trusted in our government, and it had left me unsupported and penniless. I had trusted that a job I loved and felt passionate about would last for life, and instead, my employment was cut short. I had trusted in 20 years of a rock-solid marriage, defined by love, devotion, and truth, and I was left abandoned and bereft.

Experience had taught me that I could not rely on *anything*. In fact, the only thing I could count on was that the *unexpected* would come out of nowhere and turn my beautiful, fulfilling, blessed life upside down, that life would lower the boom not once, but again and again.

In mid-August 1996 I was sitting on the sofa in my living room. The final papers for my divorce had come through in April, a death knell tolling the end of my life as I had known it. I had no one to be a mirror for me, no one to share my life with, nothing left to define me. My regular employment had fallen away, and for several months I had been scrambling internally to hold my tenuous-seeming existence together. I did not yet have a clearly conceived direction to move forward in, and I could barely make financial ends meet. During the last few days I had been experiencing sporadic panic rising out of nowhere. From time to time I could feel my heart pounding and my breath becoming shallow, and the sense of panic was so acute and disorienting that it terrified me. I tried to do everything I could to avoid it, and I reacted as many of us might in the face of rising terror: I kept myself distracted with pointless motion. I threw myself into the habitual humdrum of daily life, into rote activities that gave me some sense of normality, of security – of sanity. I took refuge in doing the things I knew I was competent at: vacuuming, cleaning, cooking, paying bills and offering my one-to-one therapies. Though occasionally I would call a friend for a chat, I felt deeply alone. I was constantly cold and no matter what I did I could not get physically warm. I was desperately trying to cobble together something that resembled my previous existence, a life that would give me some sense of connection, nourishment, and safety.

I had tried all my age-old, stalwart remedies: I took walks in nature, I meditated, chanted, and read calming words of wisdom from books by enlightened masters, but still the fear would not be assuaged. I was on the run, being hunted down, not by something outside me, but by something more immediate, more terrifying, something almost alien arising from within. I wanted to jump out of my own body to get away from it, but there was no escape. Like most of us I had fear *of* fear, and no one had given me a set of instructions marked, *What To Do in The Face of Overwhelming Fear*.

My mundane avoidance strategies and activities became increasingly ineffective at keeping the fear at bay. *Nothing* was working, and I had no idea what to do next. I caught myself vacuuming the living room carpet for the second day in a row, and I suddenly got it: I realised that I could not run anymore. I would have to face this tiger and look it in the eyes.

So I sat down and closed my eyes. Though my heart was thudding in my ears, my face was flushed hot and my breath was thin, through some force of will I turned *towards* the fear. I welcomed it to 'come and get me', and I sat still and waited. Everything seemed to swirl out of control. It felt like I was going to be pulled apart by the force of it. In my head I shouted, *"What is this fear about? What am I really afraid of?"* And I willed it to reveal itself.

The swirling chaos began to subside. Time seemed to slow down, then stand still. Eventually a reply arose within, "You're afraid that next month your ex-husband's maintenance cheque is not going to come in. You're afraid that the rug is going to be completely pulled out from under you again, and what insubstantial security you have left will be ripped from you. You are terrified that if you don't do something *now* you will be unable to pay your bills, cast out of your home, left alone and destitute."

I opened my eyes, "Shit! Is this what I'm afraid of?"

Some deep inner awareness knew that this was *exactly* what *was* going to happen – my maintenance cheque was not going to arrive – and like a good friend the fear had been trying to get my attention for days, trying to get me to wake up and take action, but I was so afraid of facing the fear that I had been on the run since the first trace of it arose, and the more I ignored it the more insistent it became. The fear was trying to warn me of what it perceived as an impending disaster, one that did in fact happen when my cheques not only failed to arrive at the end of that month, but stopped altogether.

The difficulty was that even the *unconscious* possibility of being left without my meagre financial support was so daunting, so terrifying that my mind recoiled and closed down. It was like a physical vice had clamped down on my ability to access any positive action, answers, solutions or support. I was absolutely frozen and immobilised.

Then something inside of me said, *"Stop! I am not letting this fear control me in this way!"*

And then I did a radical thing. I decided it was time to face not just this one fear about a cheque not coming in, but to face *every* fear that had ever existed, every fear that was secretly lurking inside my body, poised, ready to do its dirty work.

Taking out a spiral-bound notebook and a pen, at the top of the first page I wrote in bold, "What's The Worst That Could Happen?" as if I was calling up to the surface every fear hiding inside me. I was determined that my fears were going to come up, come out and be fully exposed. I summoned my courage and opened my being wide, as if willing the full power of these lurking fears to come to the surface, and I genuinely asked myself, "What is the worst that could happen?" genuinely wanting to know the answer. Soon I found I was dialoguing with myself.

"OK. So let's say that the cheque doesn't arrive. Then what?"

When I asked the question the panic started to arise and swirl again, but I willed myself to stay wide open in the fear, to face the naked truth of the worst that would happen.

The fear became even stronger and, as I surrendered fully to it, the next answer arose, "Well, if the cheque didn't arrive it would mean I couldn't pay my bills, couldn't afford to eat."

I felt sick at the thought of such a possibility. Fear swamped me anew as once again I asked, "OK. So if that happened, then what would happen? What's the absolute worst that would come out of that?"

Again I was awash with terrifying fear as the answer came, and the reality of it hit home. "Well, the reality is I would lose my lease and be turned out of this apartment. I would have to find shelter somewhere else, perhaps with a friend or, worse still, with my mother."

At this point a fierce pride arose and said, "No way! There is simply *no way* that at the age of 43 I am going to go cap in hand back home to my mother, to live off her like some parasite!" That meant the only option available would be to live off the generosity and kindness of my friends, something that I had always vowed I would *never, ever* do!

Suddenly the fear dissolved and I was awash with shame. When I opened and allowed all the shame of that to come flooding it swamped me completely. I felt rejected and bereft as I realised that, even with the most tolerant and loving of friends, eventually I would wear out my welcome and would have to leave. I opened once more.

This time, as I asked the question, "OK. So if that happened, that your dearest friends turned you out, *then* what's the worst that could happen?" A picture of me lying in the gutter in New York City, my hometown, arose. I was destitute, in rags, with sores on my face and with not a soul to reach out to me. I felt like I was drowning in a sea of helplessness, of hopelessness. All my education, my degrees and certifications rendered useless, like so many bits of trash. I felt I was an abject failure, and there was no hope to be found.

A part of me knew that such a ludicrous thing would never happen, and yet I was constant and determined that I would meet and face the deepest, darkest fears, no matter how ridiculous or impossible they seemed. If these fears were stored inside me, I was committed to meeting them. They were not going to run my show anymore.

So I opened completely to the truth of how appalling this picture made me feel. By this point I was lost in hopeless failure, feeling worthless, useless, and I was forced to openly confront my deepest fear head on: that I did not believe I had what it took to survive; that I was so worthless, so incapable that I just did not have the ability to take care of myself. I was beyond salvation and filled with self-disgust. I had reached rock bottom.

So I asked again, "And if this were to happen, that I would end up penniless, starving, dying in a New York City gutter, *then* what's the worst that could happen?"

Something already knew the answer, that death would come for me, and I would perish. This was the core fear at the root of it all; that because I didn't have what it takes to survive, I would die.

Again I asked, "So if you died, *then* what's the worst that could happen?"

Something inside me opened to the possibility of death. For a moment it felt as if I was being pulled apart by some unseen force, panic kept coming in waves, and I felt like I was drowning in a swirling mass of deconstruction, fighting for my life. Then eventually something quiet and still beckoned me, and invited me to stop fighting the process, even though I couldn't understand it. That same presence wordlessly invited me to let go, to surrender completely to the disorienting confusion of it all.

And something did let go. It began to feel as if everything was dissolving into a vast field of blackness. My physical form seemed to become insubstantial, non-existent, to disappear into nothingness, into pure awareness.

Everything became timeless, infinite. After some time, the awareness started transmuting into particles of light – a vast, sparkling, scintillating field of light, a presence that was *everywhere*, permeating *everything*. This field was endless, formless, and all of life was arising in it, was being embraced in it.

I experienced the whole universe as one consciousness, an all-inclusive potential waiting to manifest and express itself as form, as all of life. And I recognised that this pure potential was my own soul, my own Self. I realised that *this that I am* is permeating everything, and that all of life is occurring in me, *as* me. There is nothing separate from me, nor am I separate from anything in life.

Then came the realisation that in this potential *everything* is available: all genius, all wisdom, all love, all creativity, all answers. In fact *all of life* is born, sustained and dies away again in this vast field of unborn potential. In this presence all possibilities exist.

I sat in wonder and laughed at the ludicrous cosmic joke of it. In meeting my greatest fear – the fear of not having the ability to take care of myself, not being able to survive on my own, that I would die alone, destitute – I had fallen into my own soul. In a simple act of opening into the most frightening of possibilities, my own death, I had found liberation.

Have you ever been at an open-coffin funeral and noticed that the corpse looked like a lump of clay, devoid of whatever had been its real essence, missing whatever presence had animated it in life, lacking whatever had made it a *person*? It was the same sort of thing for me, by opening into the fear of death and surrendering to it, I experienced the body dissolving, being shed like a set of old clothes. Yet what *remained* was alive, eternal and free. It was vast, scintillating and in it all possibilities were available. All answers were right here.

Through Journeywork I had already discovered that when we fully surrender into the core of our worst, most painful and debilitating emotions, we will be carried into the core of our own being, into the enlightened, awakened presence of our essence.

But like almost all of us, when my deepest, most primal core fear was exposed, I froze. I shut down. I ran. And it was only when I stopped, turned and offered myself completely into the fear, letting it 'annihilate' me, that I was able to open freshly into the pure unbounded presence that is my own soul.

What had I been so afraid of – that I would shed some old clothing?

I was sitting there with my eyes shut, resting in this pure radiant presence, in an ocean of certain knowing that this presence was patiently waiting to use me as part of the creative solution to the impending crisis in my life. I realised it was waiting for me to call forth the answers that were there for the taking. So I opened my eyes and reached for my spiral notebook again, knowing that those old fears could no longer own me. I opened wide into this field of pure potential. Even with my eyes open it was still palpable, still vast, redolently omnipresent. And I asked, " If this infinite presence could create the highest and best in my life, what's the *best* that could happen here?"

I wrote these words at the top of a new page, and the answers started pouring onto the paper. I felt like I was a scribe for grace, my only task to keep asking, "What's the best that could happen?" letting this field of presence do all the rest. I could barely write fast enough as a new dialogue began.

"What is the best that could happen?"

"Well, I could get real and acknowledge that the cheque will probably not come, and that I need to take clear, decisive action. So the first thing I need to do is cut my bills in half, by getting a housemate who can take the second bedroom and split the rent and utility bills."

"OK, so let's say that tomorrow I go to the meditation centre and I find someone suitable who would like to share the apartment with me; then what what's the best that could come out of that?"

"I would start getting real about my general finances, and would start to budget properly. With my living expenses cut in half I could start getting creative about how to bring in more income."

"So if that happened, if I took proactive steps to increase my income, what would that look like? What's the best that could happen?"

The answers came flying out of the emptiness.

"First I would call all my friends and tell them the truth about my greatest passion in life. I would share what has happened: that since I healed from the tumour, some groundbreaking, profoundly powerful work has given birth to itself. I would share that I have been developing and refining it for the last three years and have given a few small seminars to teach the work. That the work born from my own direct experience has been effective in getting extraordinary results for others in terms of cellular healing and emotional transformation, and that people are waking up to their own magnificence. I would tell my friends, colleagues and acquaintances that I felt the new work, which I had named The Journey, would bring a whole new paradigm for natural healing to the world, and I would ask them if they might like to experience and learn how to do this new work for themselves, and if they might even be willing to host a weekend workshop in their homes or in community centres so others could benefit from it. I would finally let the secret out of the bag: that I have developed new exciting and effective work, and that I feel it is my life's calling, my destiny, to bring this work to the world."

Then I asked, "Well, if that happened, and I finally shared my passion for the work, and some people decided they wanted to host such events, then what's the best that could happen?"

"People would finally have access to these hugely transformational new tools, and would have the opportunity to experience true wholeness, freedom and healing in their lives."

"And if that happened, then what would take place next? What's the best that could happen as a result of this?"

"Those people would be so grateful to grace, to life, for the tools and process work that allowed them to experience cellular healing so effortlessly, so easily, that they would want to share this healing work with their loved ones, to help them take the lampshades off their own lives."

"So if that happened, what is the best that could take place out of that?"

"Then the waves of awakening and healing would begin to ripple out to humanity. Many seminars, larger seminars, would take place and more people, families, schools, hospitals and businesses in more countries would have access to these tools and the work would be commonly used by people from all walks of life."

"If that happened, then what would happen?"

"Books would be written to make this work accessible to people even if they couldn't get to a seminar, and people around the world would use the work to find deep wholeness, peace and abundance in their lives."

"If that happened, then what would take place? What's the best that could come out of it?"

"The media would embrace the work as a living, practical teaching, one that gets tangible, quantifiable results. It would become a mainstream paradigm for natural healing. The work would further expand, develop and deepen, and would become available in different forms; further books, CDs and DVDs would be translated into dozens of languages and would be used by many cultures and religions around the world.

"If that happened, then what's the best that could happen?"

"Journey offices would open on the various continents to make Journeywork available to everyone, to support people in their ongoing journeys. Its awakening and healing would bring people home to a true wholeness, joy and abundance that would help catalyse the shift in consciousness that our world needs. We would join a wave of awakening sweeping our planet and cause people to *wake up* to the greatness of their souls and begin living a guided life of grace."

The list went on and on, as the answers, proactive ideas and the larger vision flooded my awareness. As I looked at that list and felt the huge power of what was possible, I compared it with my list of old fears. The list of fears was *much* shorter. I asked myself, "Does this vision of possibility and action give me enough leverage to want to do a full Journey process to face and fully clear out my worst fear – of not having the ability to survive and take care of myself?"

The answer was a resounding, "YES!"

So that was what I did. I took a couple of hours with a friend and underwent a full Journey process, to clear out and finish with the old fear-consciousness. And in doing that I opened the door for all those possibilities to come true. And come true they did!

But not in the way that I expected or envisioned at that time. I could never in a million years have come up with such a graceful, all-inclusive, wholistic plan. It was as if the infinite field was a divine architect that engineered a design so wholesome and all embracing that all of life was included and held as part of the larger picture. Everything that came into its sphere of influence was encompassed in a nourishing abundance-consciousness, as if it was a living organism taking care of all of the individual parts of the whole.

Magically, wondrously, the infinite brought about the successful living manifestation of its own vision while caretaking and being a custodian of all the component parts included in that vision.

Instead of growth occurring as a linear, step-by-step, two-dimensional succession of events, expansion occurred concentrically, multi-dimensionally. Grace would create a *sphere* of abundance, embracing, flourishing each individual aspect, structure and person within that realm. Like a hologram, no matter which angle you viewed the manifestation from, it was complete, three-dimensional, whole. When expansion occurred it took place naturally, organically, in a divine timing, in response to the needs of life, and it took place *only* when it was able to sustain all of its individuals as part of the whole.

It was as if in surrendering to the infinite and by letting my actions be shaped by a more enlightened, divine inspiration, that life took care of itself every step of the way. And a new paradigm for building a conscious business emerged in the process.

I could only stand in awe of how perfectly, synchronistically, effortlessly and practically the infinite engineered the fruition of its own plan. Inspiration was always available, and I felt choicelessly guided. The results were fulfilling at every stage of the game as grace pointed me towards conscious action that produced effective and often astonishing results.

It started with the microcosm, addressing the simple needs of my little life, and moved out and began to embrace the macrocosm, all of humanity, all of life.

The day after my fear process I was guided and propelled into action. I went to my local mediation centre and found a conscious roommate who moved in that same day. The next day I started calling my friends to tell them about Journeywork. A month later I had enough workshops booked, in The States, Canada, Australia and the UK, that my schedule was full for a year.

Shortly after, I attracted a full-time business partner who had the experience and acumen to help me develop The Journey into a healthy business, and give it a corporate structure to expand internationally, to let it develop into a business that would consciously nourish and grow each person who came into its sphere of influence.

A year later, I moved to England, where the thirst for the work was fierce. Organically, exponentially the work expanded. The media got wind of it, found out that it got the results people were seeking and embraced it. In London, The Sunday Times, a highly regarded and influential newspaper, printed a hugely positive two-page-spread article, and our small organisation grew to accommodate the increasing demand. Two years later The Journey book was published, first in Britain, then Australia and South Africa – in all three countries to excellent reviews. It became a bestseller in the self-help category, remained in the top ten for several years, and is still in the top ten in a number of countries.

Offices, with staff and practitioners to guide and support people through the work, sprang up on those three continents: Europe, Australia and Africa.

And the work deepened massively, and expanded with an extensive, comprehensive course curriculum. Health professionals, doctors, teachers, businesspeople, psychologists, computer programmers, office workers, began going through the year-long, seven-course Journey Practitioner Programme, completing 45 case studies before qualifying. Therapists around the world began incorporating this work into their practices. People from all walks of life began using it as a natural part of their daily lives, and many thousands healed from life-threatening illnesses; tens of thousands awakened and began living their lives in fullness and wholeness.

The Journey attracted the attention of the international media and more than 200 articles about the work appeared in newspapers, periodicals and magazines. More than 250 radiobroadcasts have taken place, and 65 news and television programmes aired, including a couple of documentaries. The book got translated into 20 languages and over a million copies have been sold worldwide. Seminars regularly take place in more than 30 different countries, a number that grows each year.

By 1998, my business partner, Kevin Billett, whose passion for truth, love of Journeywork and commitment to serving humanity equalled my own, had become managing director of our various international companies. He also became my life partner, and we were married on the island of Maui in January of that year.

Over the next two years The Journey seminars grew exponentially, and the business expanded into a number of different countries. At each stage of the way, in every country, consciousness grew and flourished each person as part of the whole. Whenever we offered a Journey Intensive seminar, new participants were cradled and supported by trainers. They in turn received free training from me and were cosseted and guided by the depth and expertise of Journey Practitioners. In turn, the practitioners were supported in deepening in their spiritual journeys by the embrace of our international team of staff members, who themselves were personally developed, supported and flourished by our business and its directors. And in our turn Kevin and I, the custodians of this vision, were embraced by grace, guided and inspired, held and nourished as the consciousness of the organisation continued to expand to embrace humanity.

Along the way plenty of mistakes were made as we experimented with innovative new models of operation, but the generosity of the infinite field embraced those mistakes and turned them into clear, incisive lessons, making us more effective vehicles for getting the work out.

On September 10th 2001, The Journey book finally got published in the US. On September 11th the Twin Towers catastrophe occurred and, as with almost all books published in The States that month, it faded into obscurity.

Still, a small grass-roots movement began, headed up by people who had somehow obtained the book and got results. Its momentum grew, and to support the growing groundswell of demand for Journeywork, I asked our dear friends and fellow Journey Practitioners, Skip and Kristine Lackey, to open North American offices, and to offer the various foundational seminars, while I focused on the countries where The Journey was widely known and used, where the demand was greater. Slowly, organically, America began to catch on to the work, and in the last few years we have come back to the US to offer the full Journey Practitioner Programme, and Kevin's paradigm breaking Visionary Leadership Programme, which enables professionals and businesspeople to uncover and live in their authentic, conscious leadership potential, and bring this new consciousness into their corporations and organisations. Already, the number of Journey Practitioners, and Visionary Leadership Coaches is swelling in the USA and Canada, giving those countries more in-depth support in the advanced levels of the work.

In 2002 our international charitable organisation, Journey Outreach, was born with the intention of making this work available to those who would never otherwise be able to afford this kind of teaching. Today the work is offered free of charge in many ghettos, underprivileged communities, and in tribal and indigenous communities in many countries. It has been taken into orphanages, children's organisations, schools, hospitals, various religious organisations, addiction treatment centres, and prisons. Over 100 individual projects have brought this work into the lives of people who had great need of it, and who would otherwise not have had access to it. Our current projects and sponsorships run in India, South Africa, Botswana, Namibia, Kenya, Macau, Australia, New Zealand, Canada, The USA, and The Middle East. Wherever help is most needed Journey Outreach is willing to go.

Eventually, two more books were written: *The Journey for Kids – Liberating Your Child's Shining Potential*, a book based on the inspiring and heart-opening real life experiences of children finding health, wholeness and realizing their full potential; and *Freedom Is – Liberating Your Boundless Potential*, a book that gives adults practical tools for liberating their true greatness and living a life in freedom and grace.

The work kept expanding and growing, and we currently have 15 different courses available in our growing curriculum. To serve the growing demand Kevin and I now travel 44 weeks a year, giving seminars and retreats in countries all over Europe, in North America, Australia, New Zealand, South-East Asia, Japan, Africa, India and The Middle East. Still there are many more countries crying out for the work than we can get to, and in response to that call we train Journey Presenters to give the foundational work in numerous countries and in many foreign languages.

We now have four offices on four continents, with dozens of staff, associates and partners. Tens of thousands have come through the seminars over the years, and many of them have continued on to the more advanced-level retreats and have trained as trainers to support others at the events. Thousands have gone through the full Practitioner Programme, and over one thousand of those have chosen to complete the required 45 case studies and are fully qualified as Journey Practitioners.

And this is just the tip of the iceberg. All of it manifested because one day I decided to face and open into my deepest, darkest fears, and clear them out. And everything that occurred happened effortlessly, according to the infinite's perfectly designed plan. I was just a willing servant, choicelessly tethered to the divine will, guided by the power of grace.

Everything that was on that list of "The Best That Could Happen" *happened*. From the moment I decided to take the conscious action to cut my bills by getting a roommate, grace used me as a vehicle to fulfil its own prayer for this work to be used in service to humanity. And the vision became much greater than I could possibly have conceived.

I met and freed myself from those fears, and I opened into a presence of grace, a potential so profound it effortlessly flew me into motion, into conscious, effective action. And to this day I continue to be used by grace however it wishes to use me, to develop the work in whichever way it desires, and to make it available to humanity.

You are reading this book because one day I got so scared that I spontaneously fell into a process that liberated me from my worst fears. That process has now been scripted and, for the first time, is published at the back of this book for you to use. It has been refined, expanded and made more elegant and user-friendly, so you can take yourself through it, step by step, and begin living your life from the infinite field of all possibilities. This field is waiting for you, knocking on your door, beckoning you to come home to your true potential. There are billions of particles of grace with your name on them, waiting for you to open those doors, to open completely, to be used as a vehicle for conscious manifestation in your life.

It's time to wake up and expose your own worst core fear. It's time to open into it, beyond it, into the vast potential of your own soul. It's time to clear out your patterns of shutdown, finish with your stories of limitation. It's time to clear out the silent saboteurs that have been running your life and begin opening into your true potential. It's time to become part of the co-creative dance of manifestation, and to live in conscious abundance in every area of your life.

My strong suggestion to you is this: don't just think about it, *do* the work. Read the book from beginning to end, and then take yourself through the processes. Let this book be a living handbook for experiencing real freedom and abundance in your life. Just open and dive in. It's time to be part of the shift in consciousness our planet needs.

CHAPTER 2

During the last couple of decades there has been a handful of bestselling books on abundance manifestation, some of which have achieved almost a cult following. They have been loosely based on the 'father of all manifestation books', Napoleon Hill's *Think And Grow Rich*, which was originally published in 1937, although Hill's material has been rehashed in more contemporary language, couched in a more mystical or esoteric context, and synthesised to include some modern scientific findings.

The basic premise of these books is the same: according to the universe's 'Law of Attraction', if you put out focused, positive intentions – repeat positive affirmations, actively set your goals and visualise them as having already come true – then through the power of your intentions alone you can manifest your dreams. Indeed, there is research that gives weight to this principle. Modern physics proves that when you get clear about what you want and put out a strong positive intention it has a measurable effect on what manifests in your life. That old adage from The Bible, "As you think, so shall it be" has been shown to have a scientific basis.

But the unfortunate truth about most of these books is that they give us only a superficial and tiny portion of the picture. They sell us short by merely scraping the surface. *They do not address any of the deeper issues, the real underlying problems that have <u>prevented</u> us from manifesting our ideal lives.* They do not take into account the *silent saboteurs* that stop healthy manifestation from taking place even when we *have* put out strong intentions.

Such books perpetuate a myth that we can simply *imagine* our dreams into reality. And this premise appeals to the fanciful in us all. As children, we all love playing make-believe and, like Peter Pan, we so much want to believe that if we *"really, really"* see our dreams come true, *"really, really"* envision them with all our heart, then the strength of our intentions alone will be enough to make us fly. Of course it is natural that we long for life to be this magically wondrous, but eventually our common sense must see through the fallacy of such a whimsical belief. The premise is so obviously *untrue*. If it were true, then as children all our fantasies and cravings would have all been fulfilled, and as adults we would all be successful and wildly rich!

With maturity there comes a point when we have to be willing to take our heads out of the clouds. There comes a time for us to be pragmatic, and if we want to live lives rich in abundance we need to face and clear what has been *holding us back* in order to become conscious and effective co-participants in the process of *real* manifestation.

This is not to say that putting out intentions is ineffective. It can be hugely potent if those intentions come from an *authentically* positive place. It is simply that for them to produce wholesome and *consistent* results they have to be born not from some hyped-up, fear-laden fake positivity, but from an authentic, free, whole consciousness. To achieve massively healthy results we have to be congruent on *all levels of being*.

Have you ever committed to some inspiring New Year's resolutions, only to notice that three months later your resolve fizzled out and nothing much in your life seemed different? Or have you ever got specific in your goal setting, and written down your exciting intentions, then put your notes into a drawer, only to discover a year later that only a few of your goals manifested and that most did not? If putting out a strong intention and visualising those goals as if they were a reality were enough on its own, most of us would already have manifested all of our dreams. Yet most of us have not. Have your ever wondered *why* you got inconsistent results in some areas, and none in other areas?

It is because all of us harbour *silent saboteurs*, insidious killers of manifestation that often do their destructive work of shutting us down just when our full potential is beginning to burgeon. It's as if we have two simultaneous, equally potent intentions going out to life: on the one hand we say, "I'm going to manifest my dream job. I have the talent. I know I can do it!" while on the other hand we unconsciously put out the equally potent, or sometimes even stronger, negative impulse, "I'm afraid that I don't have what it takes. I don't really deserve it. I'll always be a failure." So, while your thinking mind might be artificially inducing and heightening excitement by repeating positive affirmations and visualising colourful pictures of success, and while you may be trying to force yourself, to *will* yourself into believing these pictures, at an unconscious level you remain unconvinced, and the opposite, negative impulse goes out unchecked, "I'm not good enough. This is not real. It will never happen."

As a result these polarised intentions cancel each other out. It's not that something disastrous happens; usually it's just that *nothing* happens. The potency of your positive intentions gets negated. And that is why, when you looked at your list of goals at the end of the year, only *some* of them came true, while most did not.

As long as unacknowledged fears, negative beliefs or unhealthy conditioning is within you, they will sabotage you, counter-productively affecting the wholesome goals you set.

In order to consciously and consistently manifest abundance, we *have* to be willing to *get deeply real* and actively play our part. We have to be willing to roll up our sleeves and dive in to face the unhealthy conditioning, the disempowering beliefs, vows, limitations and negative self-concepts that have insidiously prevented us from achieving the results we desired in life. Then we need to expose and penetrate the *lie* of those negativities, and clear them out.

Next we need to go deeper, to uncover the *drivers* of those negative beliefs and vows – the debilitating traumatic memories that get stored at a cellular level – and finish with them completely. Then, and only then – from a place of freedom, wholeness and pure potential – can we healthfully join in the co-creative dance of manifestation.

~

Have you ever had the experience of getting onto a new health regime; one that really excited you, one you felt passionate about? With the best of intentions you made a firm decision, "From now on I'm going to eat only healthy food, I'm going to work out regularly three times a week at the gym, and I'm going to lose twenty pounds of weight in three months. I'm determined that I'm going to get healthy and fit."

And have you ever noticed, even though you felt crystal clear in your decision, even though you felt strong and congruent in your conviction that you would follow through to the full culmination of this programme, that somehow over time your determination waned, your diet became looser and your gym routine became inconsistent then fell away entirely? That even though you were initially flying on your new health regime and felt fantastic on it, somehow you 'hit the wall' and your passion petered out. For no apparent reason you gave up doing the very thing that was giving you a renewed sense of self-confidence, and was causing you to feel more alive and on purpose. Have you ever wondered *why* that took place? It is because inside you were some hidden comfort zones that sabotaged you.

Even if this example does not specifically apply to you, I believe we have all experienced the shutdown that occurs when we start 'pushing the envelope' of our known world. When we start stretching beyond our current comfort zones, something snaps us back into limitation mode.

Athletes and sportspeople protest about this very phenomenon. They speak passionately about playing, in 'the zone', when it seemed they could do nothing wrong, when every shot or stroke seemed to come from some effortless and inspired potential, and they felt part of a greater infinite whole. For a while everything was possible and they were playing at the top of their game, then, for some unknown reason, they blew a shot, messed up, or choked, and everything went downhill. They hit the wall of their hidden comfort zones and from that point an unconscious destructive impulse incapacitated them.

Artists complain bitterly of this syndrome. For months they can be in a fire of creativity, absolutely prolific, with each new painting more inspired than the last; then one day they paint a brushstroke that seems off or uninspired, and in a heartbeat it seems that the whole of their talent deserts them. Thereafter, every new canvas is an unmitigated disaster. Sometimes these gifted artists do not come out of their slumps for months; some never come out.

The bottom line is this: they came up against the edge of their comfort zones and something in them got scared and shut down their true potential, their artistic genius.

Writers complain about 'writers' block' occurring just when the writing seems to be most inspired, and is spontaneously pouring itself onto the page, or when they win a writing contract, or get a publishing deal, and feel the increased pressure to produce quality work by a deadline. They get stopped in their tracks, their minds shut down, their creativity vaporizes and they are left staring at a blank page.

In the early days of The Journey, I did some process work with a screenwriter who had been experiencing severe depression because of this very thing. He had been commissioned to write a screenplay for a major Hollywood film studio, and for months had been staring at his computer screen trying to find a good opening and a strong story line, but was completely blocked. During his Abundance Journey process he got to the root cause of his silent saboteurs and so completely cleared out the cell memory that was driving his pattern of shutdown that from that day forward it was as if a dam broke, his creative potential became fully accessible and pure genius poured from him. He completed his screenplay in record time – he could not type fast enough to keep up with the flow of inspiration – and the film, a romantic comedy featuring A-list box-office stars, became a humungous 1990s blockbuster. Eight years later he showed up at a Journey Intensive

I gave in Los Angeles, to thank me personally. He attributed his entire success with the film to that single process.

Scientists speak of the phenomenon of their minds being wide open in an infinite field of intelligence. Einstein called it, "The still, dark place where God is", and in his experience it was the infinite that gave rise to the *Theory of Relativity*, the formula $E=MC^2$. But often scientists complain about the same syndrome that affects artists: one minute they are effortlessly working in a timeless *'Eureka!'* awareness, and the next minute a steel trap springs, shuts down their minds, and blocks their access to the genius, leaving them wallowing in uninspired, linear thought.

Some of us seem to plateau out at work. We get stuck in the complacency of rote activity, doing things the way they have always been done. Or we overreach and find our desperate need for innovation and change is unsuccessful or even counterproductive. We eventually get so mired in negativity that we cannot break free from it, and we watch less experienced, less able colleagues leapfrog over our heads to promotion after promotion, seemingly on fire with enthusiasm, inspiration and fresh ideas.

These blocks can occur in our spiritual lives. Meditators often share that they get to a stage in their meditation practice where they can no longer access the bliss and peace that they experienced in their early meditation days; they feel stuck, aware only of their incessant stream of thoughts, or they feel jaded, like they are just going through the motions.

And even in our relationships these silent saboteurs can have an undermining effect. Have you ever been in a new intimate relationship where, for a period of time you have felt open, present, accepting – perhaps more alive and in love than you have ever felt – swimming in what seemed like a divine connection that was whole and complete? And have you ever experienced that after some time, for no apparent reason, you began to feel disconnected, you suddenly closed your heart to your partner and retreated back into your shell or hid behind your protective wall, and from that defended place felt deep isolation or loneliness; all the while fiercely longing to get back to the way things were, to somehow feel once again the connectedness, the wordless, boundless intimacy that had made the relationship so sublime and fulfilling? Some silent saboteur had emerged and was doing its destructive work, and you were rendered helpless to its effects.

Comedians have their comic genius dry up. They just stop being funny and can fall into depression. Film stars, pop and rock stars – celebrated and wealthy people who seem to have truly got it made in life – often sabotage themselves with booze, drugs, or anti-social or self-destructive behaviours. Frequently, lottery winners or trust fund kids not only blow away their fortunes, but end up severely in debt. Look anywhere in life and it is not hard to find examples of people with so much to look forward to tripping themselves up, defeating themselves and falling flat on their faces.

All of us have silent saboteurs in various areas of our life, and they affect each of us in different ways at different times. Until we access what is *driving* them, they continue to shut us down just when our life seems to finally be taking off. They clip our wings and keep us grounded, incapable of soaring in our ultimate destiny.

The frustrating thing about these saboteurs is that what *drives* them is completely obscured from our conscious awareness. It is as if we have a blind spot and are unaware of what is really taking place in the depths of our being. And even though some of the beliefs and vows associated with our self-sabotaging patterns occasionally come to the surface, the root cause of them, the cell memories that give birth to those traps remain completely hidden from our view.

You might find it useful to look at it like this: We are a pond of awareness, and floating on the surface are lily pads, which are the superficial behaviours of protection and shutdown that we can clearly see. Our beliefs, vows and negative self-concepts are the stems, which are shrouded by the cover of the lily pads. And the stems, in turn, are connected to the deeper, intricate root systems that lie in the muddy silt of our unconscious, in a deeper part of our being. The roots are our own traumatic cell memories – disempowering and debilitating life experiences that have become lodged in our bodies, their negativity-consciousness alive in our cells. These are the real instigators of our hidden comfort zones, and they are the genesis of our self-sabotage. These roots give birth to our negative beliefs and internal limiting vows, and these in turn drive our destructive behaviours, the unhealthy actions that are so clearly observable at the surface.

And in order to clear our pond of awareness we have to dive beneath the surface to get access to our hidden beliefs, vows and concepts, and then go deeper still *to get to the root cause of them*. We have to uproot our old cell memories and clear them, and everything connected to them. When the entire plant is uprooted, open, clear awareness remains. And it is only from pure, unblocked, *unobscured* consciousness that a true, genuinely effective intention can be put out. Only then can that intention be unobstructed on its path to full expression, its journey to manifestation.

~

In the early years of The Journey I began to notice the destructive effects of these silent saboteurs, even though I had not yet identified what was driving them. Their existence first became blatantly apparent to me by way of a dramatic experience that happened to a dear friend of mine.

When Bill called me from Washington, DC, he was in a state of breathless excitement, "Brandon, you *are not* going to believe this, but I just had *a million dollars* invested in my business!"

"Wow, Bill – that's amazing!" I replied. I knew Bill had been trying to build his own small business, and had been struggling along on a middle-class income, just about able to cover his bills, his mortgage, and his kids' school fees, with little disposable income left over at the end of each month. One million dollars was a king's ransom to him, so I encouraged him to celebrate his good fortune, and asked him to expand on what had taken place. "That's incredible. What was that like?"

"You know, it wasn't *anything* like I expected. The terms of the deal were good, but as soon as the investors agreed to make the investment, all my fears started coming up. I started to get panic attacks, which is so unlike me! I got so scared that I went to our cabin in the woods to try to get a handle on things, and for days it seemed all my 'wealth wounds' were coming out of nowhere. I felt like I was being hunted down by demons coming from inside me. All the fears I ever had about massive abundance seemed to come at me from every direction. My imagination ran wild with all the possible catastrophes that could occur if I accepted that amount of money. I had this huge fear that if I agreed to the investment I would crash, fail miserably, and lose everything that's really important to me in life – my family might grow to despise me; my friends might reject me; ultimately I might end up with everything I love completely destroyed – all because I let someone invest in my business.

Then somehow I seemed to break through something while I was out there, and I summoned my courage, came back to DC, and signed the contract.

I honestly don't know what I was so afraid of. No disasters have happened. Nothing came crashing down. No one has turned against me or rejected me. In fact, nothing has significantly changed in my family and social life – it's just that my business has been given a boost, and has started to perform more healthily. I don't know what I was so scared about. I still live in the same home, my family still loves me, and I still have what matters most in life."

When I got off the phone, I thought, "Hmm… Bill must be really *hooked* by something deep-seated. That was an unhealthy response to what was essentially a bounteous gift from life." But I didn't give it any more thought because he had, after all, eventually been able to accept the blessing that the universe was trying to give him.

Then, three months later, I got another call from Bill. This time he was exhilarated, through the roof in his excitement. "Brandon, Brandon, you are not going to believe this! My business has grown so much in the last three months that I've won a *ten million dollar* investment for it!"

"*Ten million!?* That's phenomenal Bill. That's thrilling! What was that like?"

"Well, honestly, it was even worse than last time. I started vomiting, and the panic attacks were overwhelming. I got so terrified that I ran right back to the cabin, but this time I deliberately didn't take my cell phone with me. I had so much shit coming up that I felt like *Chicken Little* running around panicking that the sky was going to fall down. What if I couldn't make good on the investment? What if it all went down the tubes?

It was just too much good fortune to take in all at once, and I feared there must be some catch – that I was selling my soul to the devil or something. I was terrified that if I accepted the deal God would punish me, and that my whole business would collapse and I'd end up friendless and broke, with such a mountain of debt that I'd never be able to dig myself out of it.

I holed up out there in the woods, and didn't speak to anyone until the date for the investors' meeting had passed by. Then I came back to DC with my tail between my legs.

Two days later I finally pulled myself together, and I wound up the courage to call the investors to apologise and tell them what had happened – that I'd been overwhelmed by the size of the investment, and that I'd had to work out some stuff in my head. Luckily, I managed to persuade them to re-schedule the meeting, and I got the go-ahead from them; in fact the vote was unanimous.

Brandon, they put all their trust in me, all their faith in me. They believed in me – my abilities, my business acumen – more than I had believed in myself! They are sure I can create solid growth with their investment, and make it pay handsomely.

The following week the full ten million landed in my account!"

"Wow! That's an amazing story, Bill. I can't even imagine what it must have been like to see that sort of money show up in your bank account. What was that like?"

"You know what? It wasn't that big a deal. It seemed like just a bunch of numbers on a screen. I don't know what I had been so afraid of. What was that drama all about? Nothing bad happened: no catastrophes, no disasters. God hasn't struck me down, and my family hasn't stopped loving me. In fact, now the business is really taking off and everyone seems delighted!"

"That's such fabulous news, Bill, really wonderful. I'm thrilled for your family and your business, and I'm so happy to hear you are flourishing with it." I hesitated before I spoke the next sentence, "But, Bill ... as a friend ... I have to be honest with you. It sounds to me like you were really hooked by something big while you were out there in the woods. That was a pretty intense experience you just described. Frankly, it was quite an unhealthy response to a huge vote of confidence. It sounds to me like you have some deep unaddressed fears that were trying to get your attention, but you managed to override them just enough to get the investment – the truth is you didn't feel one hundred percent about accepting it; you weren't really clear on all levels of your being."

"Oh, come on, Brandon. I'm only human. You can't tell me that if someone came up to you out of the blue and dropped a million bucks in your lap it wouldn't bother you. You can't tell me that if some angel investor offered to invest ten million bucks in The Journey you wouldn't have any stuff come up – that you would just graciously accept it all and get on with your job and your life? You are not being real. It would bring up stuff for *anyone*!"

"Honestly, Bill, I don't believe I would have a problem with it. I see myself as a real *possibility thinker*. I genuinely believe that it's possible for miracles to take place in life – I've even had direct experiences of it, for goodness sakes! It's only been three years since I healed from the tumour. My *body* knows it is possible for the impossible to become manifest. I *know* that life is capable of showering all of us with grace and abundance. I honestly can't imagine that it would bother me."

There was a long pause on the line, as it seemed as if Bill was digesting my words. Then he countered with an ironic, slightly sarcastic, *"Oh really!* If you are so open to *all* possibilities, then why hasn't a million bucks been dumped into *your* lap? I'm not even going to mention the ten million."

And the comment really pissed me off! Somehow what he said *got* to me. I knew on some level of being that what he was suggesting was true; that I *did* have fears and resistances in this area. But instead of investigating it further I quickly retorted, "Bill, I really don't think I would have a problem with it."

"No? That's because life hasn't shoved it into your face, like it did with me. It hasn't *forced* you to confront your issues. Come on, just take a second here and make it real for yourself. Imagine that all your bills are completely covered – your mortgage is paid off, all your kids' school fees are covered, your automobile costs, insurances, food, clothing, and all your existing lifestyle expenses are paid – if any amount were available, how much money would you really be willing to invite into your life, let's say on a monthly basis, just for *you?"*

For a moment I superficially imagined his scenario, without taking the time to genuinely contemplate how that might feel. I answered glibly, "Honestly Bill, I'd have no problem with a large personal income. In fact, I don't think I'd have a problem with inviting *any* amount of abundance into my life." As the words left my mouth, they sounded false, even to my own ears.

"Oh, really?..." The words were dripping with sarcasm, and the rest of the reply was left dangling for a few moments, *"Then why haven't you manifested it yet?"*

When I put down the phone I felt agitated, miffed. Bill knew that I had big prayers for the growth of The Journey. He was implying that, like him, I had hidden, un-faced 'stuff', and that the only difference between us was that I was still cruising along in denial, because I had not yet been pushed beyond the edges of my comfort zone. Life had not tested me by dumping a large amount of money into my lap. He was suggesting that my issues simply had not been driven to the surface yet.

Bill knew that I had developed some powerful new work in The Journey, and he knew that the work was specifically designed to get to the root cause of our issues and clear them out. So it felt as if his words were implying that when it came to abundance I was in some spiritually superior, 'got-it-all-together' fantasyland. *And that really pissed me off* – even though a deeper part of me was beginning to suspect that there might be some truth in what he was saying.

So I decided to do an experiment, to find out the truth. I said to myself, "I'm going to ask Bill's question again, only this time I'm going to try make it as real as I can. I'm going to find out whether or not there is any truth in what he was saying. I'm going to find out whether or not I've been living life in some pseudo 'got-it-handled' arrogance.

I sat down and took a few minutes to get still and open in my being. Then I asked the question that Bill had put to me, "If all my bills were completely covered, if all my regular expenses were already paid, how much money per month would I *honestly* be comfortable to welcome – just for me?" An astronomical number immediately popped into my head, and even *I* had to admit it was ludicrous. I heard myself echoing Bill's tone with a sneering, "*Oh, really!*"

So I decided to find a way to make the scenario more real, more tangible. I got out a pen and paper and meticulously wrote down every bill I had, every payment I needed to pay each month, every regular expense I could think of. Then I said, "OK. This time I'm not going to be glib about this. If all these expenditures were completely taken care of, if I could have any amount of money per month, how much would I be willing to spend, just on me?"

I waited to hear what I would honestly admit to myself. Eventually the truthful but paltry sum arose in my awareness: $200. "Two hundred bucks! That's all?!" Here I was thinking I was this great 'possibility person' who was open to all the abundance that life has to offer, but the bottom line truth was I would only genuinely be comfortable with two hundred dollars a month to spend on myself.

I was stunned, stupefied by the truth. It caused me to stop and reappraise my supposed reality and my self-image. Then suddenly it struck me: if I looked at my annual income then deducted the total of my monthly bills, what was left over for me *personally* was *exactly two hundred dollars a month!* The appalling truth was that I had a hidden comfort zone I had been completely unaware of. As I looked back at my pattern of yearly earnings it struck me: here was a distinct pattern of self-sabotage, a cap on my income so fixed that I had *never* ventured beyond it. I had always earned a middle-income salary that varied only slightly from year to year, and every time I unconsciously began to push beyond that barrier, to break through that self-imposed lid, I had sabotaged myself.

I saw the pattern clearly, and it was shocking to admit to myself that every single time my annual income had threatened to expand beyond my comfort zone I would start pruning things back, I would cut my workload. I would cancel seminars, reasoning with myself, "You don't really need to go to Australia in the autumn and the spring, that's excessive. Once a year is enough." Or I would give myself the practical advice that my private one-to-one practice was getting too full, too time consuming, and that I needed to lighten the load, to take more time and space for myself. So I would cut back my client list and shorten my weekly schedule.

All my rational, practical-seeming career decisions had been based on what would appear to be pure common sense. But when I looked at the *whole* picture of any particular year's events I could see my entire sabotage game clearly exposed. Every time there was even the hint that my earnings would increase beyond their hidden cap, I would immediately take action to eliminate the possibility. Every time my business began to burgeon I would pull it back, so I could remain securely within some unconsciously set comfort zone.

What was worse than this discovery was the realisation that I did not have a clue what was causing me to behave this way. I thought, "Shit! Bill was absolutely right. Even though I have been experiencing only freedom and fulfilment in life, these silent saboteurs have been running my abundance show. They've been shutting me down and keeping me small, and the appalling thing is, *I didn't even know it!*"

At that moment I made a decision: no matter what it took, I would find a way to get to the bottom of my silent saboteurs and I would expose them and finish with them. And that was exactly what I did.

I began working with people on their abundance issues, and I discovered through dozens of processes with others that we *all* have hidden comfort zones in *every* area of our lives. By working directly with clients, new work organically developed; work that accurately exposed the nature of these silent saboteurs. Then, once they were uncovered, other Journey-based methods evolved to clear them out. I began to offer the Manifest Abundance retreat, so people could unearth dozens of hidden comfort zones and, by means of the new powerful and comprehensive process work, completely clear them during the course of a full weekend.

Six months after the first Abundance retreat in England, I was sitting once more with the fifty participants who had attended that seminar. (At that time I had a self-imposed rule that no more than fifty people would be allowed to attend this advanced level retreat, because I did not want large numbers of people to compromise the power and intimacy of the work, a rule that I later discovered was just another artificial ceiling, another comfort zone!)

I asked everyone to share how abundance had unfolded in their life since attending the retreat. One couple looked decidedly pleased; they had been having difficulty conceiving, and their prayer had been answered when she got pregnant *immediately* following the retreat – her big, round belly a testament to the fact. A schoolteacher who had for several years been fed up with her job at an inner city London school, had found the courage to apply for and win her dream job in a country village that she had always longed to live in. While there she had met her 'soul mate' and, at the age of thirty-three, had fallen in love for the first time. One man, a technology wiz, had found the chutzpah to take gourmet cooking classes and had developed a sideline catering business that he found deeply fulfilling.

A man who was already a financially successful business owner said, "Brandon, my abundance showed up in a different way. During the retreat, I realised that though I am blessed with a healthy monetary abundance, my success has come with a huge sacrifice to my family life. And I saw that over the years my beautiful wife and I had become strangers to one another, and that my kids are teenagers and I barely know them. Three weeks after I got home from the retreat – I assume because I had cleared so many abundance blocks – I was offered an unexpected business opportunity that would bring my company enormous financial rewards. A huge multinational conglomerate proposed a merger that would have increased my own income very significantly. Normally, my knee-jerk response would have been to jump at the opportunity, but this time I reacted differently. When I looked at the larger picture of my life and listened to my heart, I knew that I already have more than enough financial wealth. And I realised if I wanted to be truly abundant I would need to take more time to rebuild my relationships with my wife and kids; get to know them again, get close to them once more. So that's what I decided to do. I turned down the merger and have reorganised my work so that each day I have more time with my family. I finally remembered what it was that had made me fall in love with my wife in the first place. And I discovered what amazing kids I have. Now you're looking at a *truly* successful man, Brandon. I feel fully abundant in *all* areas of my life."

Everyone continued to share. Some stories were of subtle shifts, others were major life transformations. As I listened I was both inspired and a little envious.

When the meeting was over, I turned to Kevin and said, "I have to admit I'm a bit jealous. Everyone has been getting such wonderful results, in some cases dazzling results, and I'm the only one who hasn't been through the entire retreat, at least not as a student. I've been so busy developing the work and then teaching it that I haven't had the chance to experience the benefits of it. It feels out of integrity for me to be offering this work when I haven't had the chance to unearth and clear my own blocks. I want to experience the kinds of results these guys are getting!"

So, the day before the next Manifest Abundance retreat, which was taking place near Calgary, Canada, I asked Kevin to take me through the comprehensive process work from the retreat. We plunged right in.

The first stage of the abundance work ruthlessly exposes the hidden beliefs, vows, negative concepts and self-images, and hidden comfort zones that we have in all areas: relationships, finances, career, creativity, health, and so on.

As Kevin began asking me to envisage the various scenarios that were designed to push my buttons, challenge my comfort zones and bring to the surface my silent saboteurs, I noticed that some of my reactions were quite mild, while others were more palpable, more intense.

We were being extremely thorough, ruthlessly exposing numerous disempowering beliefs and limitations I had in *all* areas of abundance. Over the years of working with abundance issues, we had discovered that there was much more to working with abundance than the simplistic "Law of Attraction" principle. We realised that magnetising wealth to you was only the first of *three* stages of abundance.

It is not enough just to *attract* abundance. Once you've attained wealth in any of its various forms – new job, relationship, house, and so on, then you need to go on to address blocks to the next stage of abundance, the ability to *maintain, grow* and *flourish* the abundance that life has graced you with. It's not enough to land the perfect job, you'll need to grow with it. It's not enough to attract that ideal relationship, you'll need to take time to develop it, flourish it. It's not enough to start a new investment plan, you'll need to add to it and grow it over time.

Then Kevin and I unearthed saboteurs in the third phase of abundance – *letting abundance go* – letting it flow back out to the universe. Once abundance has flourished, there comes a time to let it go – to contribute back to life.

In this area, I uncovered a completely different set of negative beliefs and limitations than the other two areas. And once we were all done, I could see my entire "wealth psychology" clearly laid out before me, the various patterns and blocks to abundance in *all* areas of life were blatantly apparent.

It wasn't pretty.

As I had always maintained a self-image of health and freedom in the area of abundance, I was shocked to hear some of the negative beliefs that surfaced. They seemed like old voices handed down through the generations.

I realised that, even though I no longer held these beliefs to be true, they were still buried in my cells, and were still doing their destructive work. I could not believe what came cascading out of me: "I'll never amount to anything. I'm not smart enough, not good enough, not skilled enough. I'm too fat, too old to attract a worthwhile partner; no one will find me attractive. I'll never get it right; it will never be perfect enough. Life will always be a struggle. In life you just work your fingers to the bone, and then you die. There is never enough; there will never be enough. I don't deserve it; I'm not worth it. I'm useless, worthless. I'll never amount to anything. I haven't intrinsically got what it takes to make the grade. I'm a failure, a loser. I'm a fraud. I'll never really belong; I'll never be 'in with the in crowd'. I'll fail before I even attempt it; it's not even worth trying. It's greedy and ostentatious to want success, to want money. Be grateful for the simple things in life, then you won't be disappointed. Where there's simplicity, there's God..."

The list went on and on, as we dredged up all the hidden beliefs and negativities I had spent my adult life forgetting and denying. It was ugly stuff. I could barely believe that these unhealthy phrases and self-concepts belonged to me, especially since my mind and my heart seemed so free. But I soldiered on as I had committed to getting the most out of the process, no matter how uncomfortable it became.

Eventually, we came to one scenario that stopped me in my tracks. Kevin asked me to open fully and imagine it was a real-life situation, "Just imagine you could have *any* salary... What amount would you genuinely, comfortably be willing to welcome on an annual basis?"

I decided, because of my previous experience with Bill's question, that I would not treat this casually. I knew this was a sticking point for me, and I wanted to be honest and realistic. I replied, "Kev, I already know the answer to this. I know the real truth is I'm only willing to earn a modest middle-class income." I named the annual amount.

He said, "OK. So just for the sake of experiencing that you *do* have a comfort zone, imagine *doubling* that income. What would that really feel like?"

I closed my eyes for a moment, and I opened with the question, put myself into the scene and experienced it as if it were actually taking place – that my comfortable salary was doubling. My body started to contract, my throat began to constrict, my breathing became shallow and my heart started to pound. I heard myself beginning to backpedal, desperately trying to justify my need for only a modest income as a strategy to avoid facing the inexplicable out-and-out fear that was arising. "Kevin, you know, I don't believe I *need* to make more than a moderate income. I *hate* excess. I can't stand ostentation. I consider myself to be a yogi, and I prefer a Zen way of life. I like my spiritual existence; actually I admire it." My voice became shrill, and started to escalate into a shout, "If you even *try* to make me double my income *I know how to energetically block it!*"

I could not believe what was coming out of my mouth! For months I had been teaching people how to open up to the abundance of life, and I had a barrier that was so strong, so fiercely protective, that even the *thought* of expanding beyond my comfort zone was causing me to panic and spout spiritual claptrap as a defence tactic.

Kevin stood his ground, and humorously insisted that I face the fear head on. "I can't believe what I'm hearing. You wrote this stuff, you developed this work, and here you are trying to get out of facing your own issue by resorting to some sort of spiritual bullshit. You're turning into the client from hell! Now, if you are going to go through with this process, you're going to have to open and experience the full power of this comfort zone. You're going to have to open and feel whatever is here, and directly experience just how hooked you are by it." Though his words were pointed, I could sense there was also a smile in his voice.

And I heard the truth of what Kevin was saying, I fully knew that I wasn't playing by the rules. I also knew that my strategies weren't getting me anywhere, that I was just avoiding the inevitable, but I continued to backpedal for my life. *"I can't. In fact, I won't!"* I shouted.

Kevin countered more softly, more compassionately, this time, "I know you can't, but if you *could* open and feel fully, what would it *really feel like* to double that income?"

Something in his demeanour caused my resistance to soften, and I was instantly swamped with fear again. Hot tears sprang to my eyes. I felt sick.

My throat began to close down, and I felt as if I was choking. "I feel like I'm suffocating, like I'm dying. I feel like some huge catastrophe is about to take place."

"OK. So what would you have to believe in order to feel like this?"

"That if my income gets too big something dire, something dreadful is going to take place."

"And what kind of person feels like this?"

"One who is terrified of her income getting out of control. One who is stuck beyond all reason. One who can't move in this department. One who is controlled by fear."

"And what does this mean about you?"

"It means that even though I feel so free in my life in general, I am absolutely stuck, blocked in this area. I'm immobilised in fear, I'm helpless."

"What will others think about your responding in this way?"

"They'll think I'm a loser, because even though I'm teaching abundance skills to others, I can't even double my own income. They'll think I'm a fraud."

"And what does that mean about life?" Kevin finally asked.

"That it's only okay to live life to a limited level. But if you take just *one* step beyond that ceiling you're going to die, or something terrible is going to happen. It means that life is not as expansive as I thought; that it's limited by the fears that paralyse and control me."

I looked at what we had written down, and was astonished by, first, how hooked I was and, second, what incredibly unhealthy beliefs were attached to this bizarre and inexplicable lid I had put on my income.

By this time we had unearthed numerous other comfort zones, but it was crystal clear that this was the one I would have to work with. It was far and away the strongest, most painful hook. So we decided to use it as our starting place for the next stage of the Abundance Journey process, which would involve opening into this fear and going right into the core of it, right through the emotional layers to open into my very essence, my soul. From that level of being we would be able to turn the flashlight on and expose the root cause of not only this comfort zone, but all the negative beliefs, concepts and saboteurs.

We were going to dive into the pond, past the stems of negative beliefs, into the root system of it all. And from the deepest level, the level of infinite intelligence, we would go through the process of clearing out the core of this issue. So Kevin asked me to once again close my eyes and imagine doubling my comfortable income, and to welcome the fears associated with that.

Again my body started closing down, my throat clenched and a wave of nausea washed over me. I was sick with fear as my throat became even more constricted, like I was suffocating, as if I was being strangled. I felt like I might die.

"So what are you feeling?"

"All-consuming fear. Paralysing fear."

"Surround this fear with your own acceptance and embrace it with love... and now open into the very core of it and just stay there... So what's here in the core of this fear?"

I felt my being open to embrace the fear, and went directly into the centre of it. It was like the heart-thudding fear of a cornered animal; one that knows it is trapped and knows there is no escape. As I sat still in the core of it, my fear began to transmute, and I felt helpless. Hopelessness overwhelmed me. I knew no more options were available: I was going to die.

"Hopelessness", I said. "Devastation... It's like I'm going to die."

Kevin said, "So open even deeper into that feeling. Welcome it all. Just make sure you stay with the process and what is coming up for you emotionally. And as we open through the emotional layers, if at any point along the way a scene or picture or memory arises, just let me know."

At that moment a picture arose in my awareness. It was a memory I had not thought about in years: it was my first month at university, and I had come home to visit my parents for the weekend. I briefly shared the memory with Kevin, and he noted it down reminding me to stay with the emotion, and that we would come back to the memory later.

"Just let the hopeless devastation overwhelm you... What's in the core of it?"

I surrendered into the core of it, and let it 'have me'. It began to feel like I was dying, that some sort of death was taking place. Everything turned black.

"Death... Blackness" I replied, "Nothing... Complete emptiness."

"And what's in the very core of this nothing, this complete emptiness? What's in the heart of it?"

I let go even more deeply, and everything started becoming light. "It's turning into light", I said, "It's light!"

"And what's in the heart of this light? What is its essence?"

The light began expanding. Everything was an infinite field of all life. And I was aware that all abundance was intrinsic to this field. I said, "I'm everything, everywhere... I'm love... I'm infinite... I'm all abundance."

Just by opening down through the emotional layers, I had opened into my own soul, which I realised was everywhere, in everything. The layers were:

Overwhelming fear

Hopelessness... devastation

Death... blackness... emptiness

Light... love

Infinite everything: my own essence... life itself... infinite abundance.

We rested in this vast potential for some moments before Kevin continued with the process and invited me to start going back *up* through the levels. He asked, "If this infinite potential, this field of love that is all-pervasive, omnipresent, had anything to say to the previous level of death and blackness, what would it say?"

The answer came spontaneously from the depths of this field, "Death is natural, just a letting go, a transition."

"So let this consciousness of infinite love, pure potential, wash through and dissolve that old layer of death, of blackness... letting it be bathed in the light, dissolving into the presence of grace."

I let this happen, and heard Kevin say, "And knowing yourself to be everything, everywhere, this that is *all* of life... if this ocean of love had something to say to the next level up, the hopeless devastation, what would it say?"

"It would say, "Stop fighting. Let yourself *be* devastated. Surrender to it." I felt how natural and easy that was.

"Now let this infinite potential wash through and dissolve that old consciousness of devastation", Kevin continued. And as I did that, the devastation merged into the infinite.

Kevin then reminded me that this was the level at which the cell memory had shown up. He said, "This was the level where that picture arose, so this will be the place where we can address that old memory, and finish with it. So, right here, just imagine a campfire... The nature of this campfire is pure acceptance, unconditional love... And to this fire I'd like to ask you to bring the younger 18-year-old you, the one from your memory, the one who was in her first month at college... Then I'd like to ask you to invite the present-day you, the one sitting right here in this chair... Now welcome a mentor, one whose wisdom you trust: it could be a sage, a saint, or an enlightened master. It can be someone real, or someone born from your own imagination. It is someone in whose presence you feel safe, someone whose guidance you trust."

The younger me appeared before me in my mind's eye. She was looking strained, haunted. Then the present me showed up. Then the mentor appeared: an enlightened master I had sat with.

Kevin asked, "Who else was in the memory? Who else needs to be at this campfire?"

"Well, my Mum and Dad were there." At that point, the whole memory suddenly came flooding at once. It was as if it was occurring right then and there, in living colour.

After three weeks at college, I came home for the weekend for my first visit with my parents. The house was in turmoil. It felt like a black cloud had descended on it – again. Dad was in one of his debilitating dark depressions.

Throughout my life I had witnessed my father go through a series of nervous breakdowns, as he collapsed under the impossible pressure of his job responsibilities. He worked for General Electric, in a division that was contracted to the US Department of Defence, as an electrical engineer who designed multi-million dollar radar systems to detect possible incoming missiles during The Cold War. In his department he was the chief inventor and designer, and he felt the enormous weight of responsibility for these huge and vitally important projects. The fear that his calculations might contain a single error that would incapacitate a whole system, that his designs might be flawed and could malfunction, kept him awake night after night. For weeks on end he would stay up until 4:00 AM, sitting at his desk, pouring over the hundreds of pages of calculations that were the 'think-tank' computer printouts of his designs, trying to find any potential miscalculation in a morass of numbers. His mind would sift through pages and pages of data, seeking that one possible error in an endless sea of digits. He was frantic at the thought of what a mistake might cost his company, and he became desperate whenever he contemplated what his failure might one day cost in American lives. The safety of his country was a goal that relentlessly drove him every day, and the weight of it crushed his spirit every night.

As an inventor, my father was a bona fide genius, but at heart he was a humble, modest man. Taking on the responsibility for heading up both the design and the construction of the radar systems was a pressure too great for his shoulders to bear. Yet his company knew that they needed him to fulfil both aspects of the projects. Not only did they need him to design these intricate radar systems, but for them to be successfully constructed they needed him to manage the teams that built them. Inevitably, they would try to seduce him by offering him a modest bonus if he would just agree to work at some Department of Defence site – maybe at The Pentagon, maybe in the military eavesdropping site in Tully, Greenland – for some months to see one more top-secret project through to its completion.

Though my father had a brilliant mind, he was not a leader among men. I would watch him waiver, trying in vain to resist the pressure. He knew that if he took on another full project he would be overseeing 400 people, and he knew that the pressure would probably be too much to bear, that he would likely crumble under the weight of it. But he also knew that the extra money he would earn could make it possible for our family to get by a little easier, make us a bit more financially secure.

Like everyone in our neighbourhood, it seemed our family was always obsessed with a "What will the neighbours think?" mentality. It was as if we were continually struggling to 'keep up with the Joneses'. Our modest middle-class standard of living was never enough. We were always striving to live the American Dream: to upgrade to a better model car; to have a fancier Fridge in our kitchen; to wear the latest designer clothes; to buy the expensive full-season ski passes. If my father took on the job with its commensurate bonus, then we would take one more step up the invisible ladder that belonged to those ubiquitous Joneses.

Of course, Dad would eventually succumb and agree, and we would inevitably get the dreaded phone call from the hospital: Dad was once again suffering from a nervous breakdown after working day and night for months on end. They would send him home a hollow shell of the man who had left, and he would always swear to us all that he would never again agree to manage those projects. But within another few years, the social and financial pressure would have built sufficiently for him to give in, and the whole unhealthy cycle would start over again.

When I came home from university that weekend, Dad was once again in a black hole of despair. He was frantically desperate. He was in the final completion stages of a project design, and his 'needle in the haystack' obsession was operating in full force.

I lay awake in bed on Saturday night, listening to my parents arguing. Mum was badgering Dad, trying to get him to stop obsessing, to be less of a perfectionist. Her words seemed only to drive him deeper into despair. It was one of those pointless, futile fights that leads nowhere and exhausts both parties, leaving them estranged and defensive. Dad went back into his study, put the 'Top Secret' sign on his door and buried himself in his printouts again.

On Sunday morning there was a pall over the house. Dad looked hollow-eyed and grey, his nerves frayed to breaking point. After breakfast, I decided that I would try to reach out to him, somehow try to penetrate the haze of his desperation. So I came up with a plan to leave a note of comfort and support on his desk. After he had drunk his coffee he would undoubtedly head straight back into his study, and before he got swamped in a sea of calculations, he might pause for a moment to read my note. Maybe it would get under his guard, and perhaps he would find some comfort in it. So I wrote:

"Dear Daddy,
It seems that once again you are being burdened by the immense responsibility of your work. I'm aware that you are in one of your deep depressions, Daddy, and I just wish there was a way you could offer at least *some* of your burden up to God. You seem so weighed down. I wish you could share some of this weight, so you wouldn't have to shoulder it all on your own..."

At 11:30 AM Dad came out of his study clutching the note. He was hollowed out, frantic, wild-eyed. He seemed somehow insubstantial, almost transparent. With a hand that was shaking like a palsy he held up my note, and in a harsh, accusatory tone demanded, *"What does this mean?... Give up my burden to God? What exactly do you mean by this?"*

"Daddy... I don't know... You seem so weighed down, and I just wanted to help. I just felt that if you could somehow trust God, or somehow give the burden up to grace, maybe it wouldn't be such a heavy weight for you to carry all alone."

"Yes, you said that in the letter. *But what do you <u>mean</u>* 'give my burden up to God'?" His eyes were crazed with anguish. He looked like a demented hunted animal.

I started to stumble, to stutter, "I... I... I don't know Daddy... I don't know how to describe it... I just... I thought that if you could somehow *know* that there was someone, 'something' out there to share your burden with you... maybe you wouldn't feel so..." My sentence fell away, as I sensed the futility of my effort to explain exactly what I meant.

I longed so much to reach out to him, to touch him, to reassure him with some wordless gesture. I took a step forward and reached out to embrace him. He flinched and backed away at my touch. He looked at me in disbelief, as if I had asked him to commit some heinous crime. He seemed crushed, broken. He shook his head as if in abject defeat. He turned and walked back into his study, and he shut the door.

That touch: it felt like he was made of air, like there was nothing to him, as if he were a ghost. That contemptuous glance: it would burn itself into my memory forever. That desperate, anguished conversation was the last I would ever have with my father.

I got on the bus back to university, and arrived two hours later. When I stepped into my dorm room the phone was ringing insistently. It was my elder brother Chris. In an impossibly icy voice, he told me to sit down. I was annoyed by his tone and told him to stop being so melodramatic, to just spit it out, "Just say what you have to say, for goodness sakes."

Like cold steel he commanded me, "Sit down!" And he bluntly shared the news. Dad had gone to work, and had handed in his perfectly designed radar system. He had returned home while Mum was still out shopping, taken some rope, tied a perfect noose, and had hanged himself.

Linny, my eleven-year-old little sister had been the first to open the garage door. Daddy was still warm when she found him. She was only minutes, perhaps just seconds too late. She ran to find Chris.

In a clinical, detached voice, Chris related how he had got a ladder and cut him down. As I listened on the phone it seemed like the words were coming through some distant hollow tunnel. This *could not* be true – this was someone else's nightmare, not mine.

My father's feverish eyes flashed before me. I saw again his frantic anguish, the look of betrayal as he asked me, "What do you mean *give my burden up to God? What do you mean by this?!*" The scene played over and over in front of my eyes, until a dreadful realisation dawned: he had mistaken what I meant. He had *literally* given his burden up to God. My beloved father had committed suicide because of my stupid, misguided note. I was responsible for his death.

My world caved in. A steel door slammed shut around my heart.

I got life's deeper message loud and clear, "Oh, it's OK to make a nice, safe, middle-class income, but boy, you stretch to get that bonus, you pressure yourself to earn that little bit extra, and it will kill you – or you'll end up responsible for killing someone else, someone you love."

In that instant I made a hard and fast vow: I would *never, ever* make a big income. I would never again be responsible for anyone's death. The vow got burned into my cells. And although over time I had totally forgotten the vow, it had continued to limit and sabotage me financially, right up to the time of this Journey process. Though I had *no current* knowledge of it, the vow had had a destructive life of its own with regard to my own personal finances.

And guess how much my current income was? It was the contemporary equivalent of what my father had earned before bonuses. My body had been fighting for its life to make sure I didn't earn one dollar more than my self-imposed lid. So when Kevin asked me to double that moderate income, he was asking my body to do something it had vowed *never* to do. He did not realise it, but he was asking me to risk death.

I was stunned by the revelation. Never in a million years could I have imagined that these two issues were linked – that my father's suicide was the root cause of my abundance issue. I would *never* have been able to figure out that having anything more than an average middle-class income was inextricably wired inside me as being equivalent to death. My salary limitation had *literally* been a life-or-death matter.

In the openness of the Abundance Journey process, I saw through the lie of *all* my excuses, my arrogant beliefs and pseudo-spiritual aphorisms. None of them had any truth. None of them had any validity whatsoever. They were just part of the mechanism of my cover-up job.

I had spent my whole adult life creating an identity that fitted into and conformed to a set comfort zone, with a finite lid. And it had all been caused and perpetuated by that devastating cell memory. That memory was at the very root of my entire limited abundance-consciousness.

In my proces, I was still at the campfire stage, and my soul had already revealed the genesis of my abundance issues. I still needed to go through the rest of the housecleaning segments of the session; I needed to penetrate any remaining lies and clear out any residual or connected issues. I needed to clear out the old negative beliefs and replace them with new, healthy, supportive ones; beliefs that would empower me to begin living in a lid-free abundance-consciousness.

So, Kevin continued leading me through the campfire process. He suggested that I invite my father and my mother to come sit with me at the fire. Beginning with the younger me, he asked me to empty out all the unspoken, unacknowledged pain, to verbalise out loud the words I had never gotten a chance to say; words that had been buried within me ever since I was first frozen and numbed by the news I heard in my dorm room. He encouraged me to empty out all the stored consciousness of that memory, to get it off my chest and out of my cells.

There were mountains of guilt that needed to be expressed; tears of grief, helplessness and, ultimately, a deep longing to be forgiven for having been so foolhardy as to write a note that would end up being the final straw for my father, a note that may have tipped him over the edge.

When I had fully and completely expressed what had for my whole adult life been buried, inaccessible and hence inexpressible, I felt naturally empty, washed clean and still.

Kevin then invited me to welcome Dad to dialogue with me, to share what had been going on for him at that time, and to empty out the truth of his own experience. In listening to my father, I became aware for the first time that his death was not my fault. He confided that he had been frantically searching for someone or something to confirm what he was already planning to do. He had been looking for a sign that he should end the pain by ending his life. He just could not take the crushing pressure of life anymore. He could not bear another day of devastating anguish. So he took my note as the sign, as the confirmation for a decision that essentially had already been made.

At the campfire he made it patently clear that *I was not to blame*, that I was not responsible for a lifetime's pain that had brought him to this desperate point. I had served as a contributory catalyst for that final action, but I had *not* been its cause.

I asked him to forgive me for my part in it, and wholeheartedly all forgiveness came my way. My heart exploded in gratitude. Then Dad asked me to forgive him for taking his own life and for abandoning our family and leaving us bereft, and my heart opened as an overwhelming forgiveness flooded back to him.

There were a lot of tears, a lot of empathy, a lot of understanding, and by the end, deep relief and full completion. I was finally and completely free from the memory and the consciousness that had shut me down and kept me limited for more than twenty-five years.

Kevin and I continued with the rest of the comprehensive sweep-clean, clearing other related cell memories and other unwholesome beliefs and vows until, at the end, I was completely cleaned out and wide open in consciousness. I was left vast, whole, and ready to begin living my life from a healthy abundance-consciousness. I was free to be part of the co-creative dance of manifestation.

When I opened my eyes everything looked different, as if all of *life* had been washed clean, as if some invisible veil had been lifted from my eyes. Everything was so vivid, so alive. Colours seemed impossibly bright and all of life seemed imbued with a scintillating, sparkling presence.

In really getting to the root system under my lily pad, and uprooting the whole plant – roots, stems, pads and all – all that remained was the clear unobscured pond of consciousness. It was as if the universe had handed me a blank canvas and invited me to paint my life anew.

After the process was finished, when I inquired how much income I would genuinely be willing to welcome into my life, the answer was entirely open-ended, "As much as life wants to shower and bless me with! As much as is needed to support my prayer for this work to get out to humanity. A limitless amount."

It seemed that all my internal doors had been flung wide open to life, and I was welcoming in all those billions of particles of grace that had my name on them. I was saying a resounding "Yes!" to life. For the first time ever, I was welcoming all abundance, in all its forms. I was saying to life, "Use me however you will to fulfil whatever destiny is in store here. Let me flow into conscious action. Let me participate as part of the infinite plan to create abundance in this life."

From that moment on, The Journey organisation took off. With the lid taken off, Kevin and I were able to open ourselves to be fully used by grace. Whatever abundance was needed to get the work out there flooded in naturally. It also flowed back out naturally to serve and support the participants in learning and experiencing the work. The Journey continued to expand: organically, according to the will of life and with distinctly divine timing. It grew to the degree that it could take care of everyone involved in it, to the extent that it could healthily, wholesomely look after all its components, and always according to the will of a purpose greater than itself.

Over the years I've undergone this hugely clearing process again and again, each time exposing different specific silent saboteurs, beliefs, vows, hidden comfort zones and cell memories and clearing them out. As the veils have fallen away, more and more of *this that I am* has been exposed. More of this unborn potential, this field of all possibilities has been made available. I've been freed up to participate in co-creating abundance through conscious action, and more doors have opened to allow healthy abundance to flow freely into all areas of my life and out again.

For the first time, the full Abundance Journey process is published here and is available for your own use. It is included in the last chapter of this book. Please know that each time you undergo the Abundance Journey process you will get to the root cell memories connected to specific patterns of shutdown. You will uncover the *specific* drivers of silent saboteurs and comfort zones. But rarely, if ever, are those cell memories as intensely dramatic, as seemingly life threatening, as that original memory was for me.

Generally our cell memories are more subtle. And yet, often the most insignificant-seeming of memories can have the most destructive and farthest-reaching effects. In my work with other people over the years, I have been stunned to observe how some simple-seeming cell memories can be the root of a huge pattern of self-sabotage.

The memories can seem fairly innocuous. Maybe in school you were hauled to the front of the class and humiliated for not completing your homework on time. Perhaps you failed an exam that your friends all aced. You may have been harshly berated or judged by a teacher or a fellow student, for failing to understand a theoretical concept or a mathematical formula. Maybe you tried to give a recital or presentation and went blank in front of your audience, and ran off stage feeling like a complete fool. You may have become injured while playing a sport when you felt you were at your peak, or just before a big game. Maybe you just got cut from the team. You may have lost a grandparent or other relative at a time when you needed their support or guidance. Perhaps your college of first choice turned you down. Or maybe your first love fell in love with your best friend and dumped you. Maybe you messed up a job interview and the position went to someone less capable than you. On and on; any one of these kinds of normal every-day events can lead to the creation of negative beliefs and comfort zones which can eventually have a destructive effect, shut us down, and sabotage some aspect of our life.

With the Abundance Journey process you can really get to the bottom of these root cell memories, whatever they are, and you can clear out the limiting consciousness so completely, that it will open the door and allow full abundance-consciousness to flood into your life. With this work you have the *tools* you need to open into your greatness, to access the full expression of your true potential. Doing this work will open you to begin living from your own full potential, and allow you to be part of the healthy co-creative dance of manifestation.

The field of abundance *wants* to use you. It wants to use *all* of you, as part of the flow of creative abundance. And with this process work, all of what you truly are in your essence becomes available. From this vast potential, true genius, talent, creativity, answers and inspiration will arise. And as it flows you into conscious, healthy action, you will feel in each moment the deep fulfilment of letting all of yourself be lived by life. For life is inviting us to play a larger role, to step up to the plate. It is no longer okay just to get by – *life* needs our greatness to help make the shift in consciousness that *our planet* needs.

We are at a time when creative genius is needed, when truly inspired answers are being called forth, and where conscious action is being demanded. In Barack Obama's inaugural Presidential speech he invited all Americans to take responsibility for themselves and for the changes that are necessary in society and in the world. He told us that anything is possible. This process work gives you the ability to unveil the field of all possibilities, for you to let your greatness shine. It opens you into your own genius, and it will allow you to participate wholesomely in creating the conscious abundance that the whole world needs.

Your life can become a living transmission of abundance-consciousness, a force that will inspire others to find the same possibility within themselves. Like Mahatma Gandhi, Martin Luther King Jr., and Nelson Mandela, your consciousness can be a living presence that has a transforming, a transmuting effect on those around you.

So as you go through the work, bear in mind the larger picture; that together we can *be* the change our planet needs. Your time for greatness is here, as is ours, and it is time we respond to this global imperative.

CHAPTER 3

Negative Beliefs

As we have learned from Brandon's illustrations in the last chapters, when we are willing to truly stop and be still we can use some simple yet powerful process work to open deeper than our thinking mind, into an expansive awareness that will lay our self-sabotaging patterns bare. Then, from this pure consciousness we can begin dealing effectively with the root causes of our unhealthy behaviours, instead of tinkering with their surface symptoms.

It is from this same vast openness that we can unearth and clear out the stems of our issues: the negative beliefs that can insidiously undermine our authentic self-confidence and positivity.

Inter-generational and Stacked Beliefs

These beliefs may have been unhealthy for us from the start, they may have compromised us since the day of their inception, or they may have begun in a more neutral or even positive fashion and then *become* unsupportive over time, as we grew and matured as beings. They may have come from our own life experience or have been handed down from previous generations. A negative belief may act as a sole agent, creating over time a pattern of limitation – we saw an example of this with Brandon's, "I don't have what it takes to survive on my own" belief, and the eventual results it catalysed – and more often we find that beliefs stack up and combine in an amalgam to cause a variety of unwholesome behaviours.

For many decades my own family lived with unhealthy stacked beliefs – beliefs handed down through the previous generation on my paternal side, which were added to and strengthened by our own direct experiences. They shaped up something like this: "Our working class background is an inescapable part of us, it is in our blood. We have to work harder than everyone else in order to better ourselves and 'prove' our worth. We will never have enough money to be truly comfortable or secure. Whatever we do achieve is always at risk – it can and probably will be snatched away when we least expect it".

These beliefs were interrelated and mutually reinforcing, and though they were not openly admitted, nor spoken about directly, their existence was obvious and was alluded to repeatedly in family conversations.

When I first started using the Abundance Journey process, my generational beliefs became very clear, as did the sabotaging effect they had been having on my own behaviours throughout life. And though my patterns – of fearful insecurity, wilful effort and low self-esteem – were different from Brandon's, the results in some respects were similar: for decades I failed to find true fulfilment and did not create the wholesome abundance in life that I longed for.

I was born in the poor coalmining valley of Rhondda, in Wales. My father was a coalminer, and my mother an office clerk. They had been brought up in the 1930s and during WWII, when food, clothing and basic provisions were all scarce. My parents had been instilled with a fear of lack, and their fears had over the years become beliefs that this lack was a permanent undercurrent of life.

Mum and Dad longed to break free, both financially and from the oppressive economic limitations of the area in which we lived. They studied in night school: Mum became a hair stylist and started her own small business, and Dad qualified as a mining engineer, and got a promotion. Then, *just as our family income was getting healthier*, there was an explosion in Dad's coalmine, and many of his friends and co-workers were either killed or horribly burnt by the blast. Though Dad was not physically hurt, the trauma of the disaster badly affected him, and when, some eighteen months later, he was buried underground by a collapse of coal and had to be dug out and rescued, he and Mum felt that the writing was on the wall – they did not want to risk a 'three strikes; you're out' scenario – and they decided Dad would need to find another career.

What they had learned from this; what got added to their stack of beliefs was: Success is transient. Even when you *seem* to be getting ahead, catastrophe is always waiting, ready to strike.

Dad interviewed for several jobs, and eventually agreed to start as a salesman with an electrical appliances company. The day before he was due to start his new work, Mum approached Dad and said, "John, I think you'd better speak to my father."

"Why is that, Luv?" he asked.

"I'm not sure... I think he wants to offer you a job."

Mum's father, Papa, had over many years developed a hobby of watch and clock repairing into a modest retail business. He now owned three small stores in mining communities, selling watches, clocks and a small amount of modestly priced jewellery. He offered Dad a job as manager of one of these small shops.

Though the salary was much less than my father had been accustomed to, the opportunity to learn the craft of horology, and the chance to earn increasing commissions by developing a business on his own won him over, and he started with Papa. For six years Dad put huge amounts of enthusiasm, time and energy into the shop, and it developed into a thriving small business. His commissions climbed each year. Mum also worked hard for long hours in her hair styling business and that flourished too. Our family income increased, and for the first time we were able to afford a small brand new car – one that could just fit the three of us plus my newborn sister, Debs.

Eventually, my parents' dream of escaping the clutches of the coalmining valley was realised, and when I was nine years old, we moved to a new modest-size home in The Vale, where it was cleaner, greener, more up-market and affluent. My first abundance lesson came quickly thereafter.

I had no appreciation at that time how much of a step up the social ladder that move seemed to my parents. I had no idea that they felt insecure, out of their depth, in moving to a more upmarket community. And I had no clue how undermined they were by their stacked beliefs about their background and the class we came from – but I was about to find out.

On my first day at my new school, I dressed in my normal school clothes, short trousers, a shirt and a pullover, and I marched enthusiastically downstairs. I was met with disapproving looks from both my parents.

"That won't do", said Dad. "Go back upstairs and put on a suit, one of the ones you wear to church on Sundays, and find a shirt and tie to go with it. You need to make a good impression. We're in a new place now, and no son of mine is going to school dressed like a ragamuffin."

"But Dad..." I complained.

"No 'buts' about it", he replied. "Now put on a suit."

I looked at Mum for support, but she offered none. She turned her head toward the stairs and flicked her eyes upwards indicating that I should shut up and comply. My heart sank at the thought of meeting new friends and new teachers trussed up in my 'Sunday best' suit and tie. Would everyone else be dressed as formally, I wondered, or would I be the odd one out?

Dad drove me to school, and as we approached the gates I became horrified to see that other kids were coming to school in casual clothes: jeans, slacks, polo shirts and sweaters; normal stuff, like I usually wore to school. I felt wrong-footed, out of place, stupid, and I teared up as I stepped out of the car. My humiliation was complete when the teacher called me to the front of the classroom and introduced me to my new classmates. I got looks of astonishment from every kid in the class, and they giggled in bemusement that any student would actually turn up for school in a suit and tie – especially one that had just moved in from a poor, working-class coalmining town.

In my acute discomfort the harsh truth seeped in, and my own version of our family's unworthiness belief took root: "You're a valleys boy. You're out of your class here. In fact, you're so out of your depth that you have to *pretend* to be something you're not. But however much you dress up, however much you fake it, you'll never be one of these kids – you'll never be good enough, you'll never really fit in".

It took weeks of persuasion, of cajoling with every argument I could muster, before Dad and Mum agreed that I could attend school dressed the same way as the other children. But even though my belief had proven untrue – I quickly made good friends and was accepted on equal terms by my classmates – it had already crept under my guard and had lodged in my cells: "Because of who your family is and where you were born, you are worth less than those from more privileged backgrounds. Though you may succeed financially in life, you will never be able to rub out the stain of your working-class roots".

We soon settled into our new community. When Dad's little jewellery shop continued to flourish my mother joined him there, and together they worked to grow the business. Their commissions grew until, eighteen months later, there was a family fracas. It was Christmas Day, and the season's sales had been excellent. Mum and Dad sat down with my grandfather to figure out the commissions they were due, and an argument broke out. Papa felt that their bonuses had become too high, and he wanted to adjust the rate downwards. My mother sat in silent hurt, but my father was explosively indignant.

"We built that shop from almost nothing. We deserve every penny we've earned. If that's the way you want it, you can find someone else to run your shop!" Dad shouted at his father-in-law. "We'll buy our own shop."

"Fine!" retorted Papa. "Why don't you do that? In fact, if you're serious you can buy this one. I'll sell it to you."

"Okay. You're on." My father shot back. And in a rather acrimonious atmosphere the deal was done. A price was negotiated, a term of repayment agreed, and within a few weeks my parents had stepped up from being store managers to store owners, bona fide businesspeople.

They decided to upgrade the shop, so they approached their bank manager and secured a loan to remodel the storefront and to buy new window displays. They negotiated larger credit and longer terms with their suppliers so they could increase the volume and the quality of their stock, and they worked their butts off. They staffed the store 9:00 to 5:30 each day, then after hours would visit wholesalers to replenish the shelves, and would attend to the paperwork and accounting. Dad would work late into the nights repairing watches and clocks, and their business grew.

Everything seemed to be going smoothly, until one morning when I woke up bleary-eyed and trudged downstairs to get breakfast. I heard hushed voices coming from the living room and went to investigate. On the sofa sat both my grandparents, and in the armchairs sat Mum and Dad. She looked distraught, and had been crying. He looked grey, shell-shocked and stunned. It felt like a funeral, like someone had died. For a moment, no one spoke.

"What's the matter?" I asked, as I walked over to Mum and sat on the arm of her chair. "What has happened?"

"It's the shop", she replied. "It burned down last night. There's nothing left, just some rubble and a burnt out shell, and we have almost no insurance, so we don't know what to do."

My grandparents offered consoling words as my parents sat silently contemplating the enormity of their difficulty: they had borrowed heavily to upgrade and restock the shop; they had loans from the bank; they had unpaid credit with suppliers, and an amount still outstanding to Papa – and they had no way to repay any of it. They had a mortgage and two kids, they had bills to pay, but they had no income and no way to make one.

Once again life's lesson was clear, and the belief became more deeply ingrained in us all: "You may *think* you're succeeding, you may *think* all your hard work is paying off, but it is not. When you least expect it, it will all be taken from you, it will all go up in smoke".

Through the goodwill of others and their own effort and dedication, my parents found a way to rebuild the shop, and grow the business once again, but our underlying fearful beliefs continued to wield an unforgiving axe on our family's fortunes, and drove ongoing cycles of success followed by crashing failures.

Eventually, I went to university and got a degree in economics. I learned about business management, finance and banking, and I joined the family jewellery business, which was now a small but healthy chain of retail stores. I continued to study topics I was sure would bring success and wealth. I read countless books and listened endlessly to audiotapes on personal growth, management and business building. I turned into a workaholic, vowing that by the time I was thirty-five years old I would have a perfect wife, a big house on the beach and a Ferrari on the driveway. I strove desperately to break the shackles of my past, to make it, to be a success.

And for a while it seemed to work – some new technique or strategy would seem to pay dividends. But ultimately, my experience was the same as my parents' had been. Whenever there was a period of success and growth, the axe would fall and bring it crashing back down: a recession would bring sales of jewellery to a grinding halt; development cost overruns would be financially crippling; family illnesses would leave us traumatised, incapacitated. And eventually, whenever there was a period of expansion and success some fearful discomfort would arise in my body, and I would feel like I was skating on thin ice, that it was dangerous territory. I had become negatively conditioned to unconsciously fear success.

The family business continued in its boom and bust cycles, until it eventually failed entirely and was liquidated. Our stacked negative beliefs had turned into a legacy from which there seemed to be no escape.

But, several years later, it took just one Abundance Journey process to cut right through that legacy, and finish it completely. By doing the same work that this book invites you to do – opening into unbounded consciousness, facing my fears unearthing the cell memories, discovering the linked beliefs; and clearing them all out – the unhealthy cycles of my past stopped right there. I freed myself to live a life of open and wholesome abundance, to joyfully embrace all that life has to offer, and to allow our Journey businesses to healthfully flourish. And more than this, I finished the painful cycle: I stopped unconsciously passing on my family's old negative beliefs to the next generation, to my own sons and nephews.

Collective Beliefs

There are many different types of sabotaging beliefs, and their variety never ceases to amaze us at Abundance retreats. Some can be individual while others, as we have seen, can be inherited family traditions. There are also beliefs that are much wider based, and some of them are so pervasive that we might even overlook, viewing them as a simple fact of life. From the moment we are born we become immersed in a collective belief-ridden consciousness: societal beliefs; class beliefs; national identity beliefs; sexual and gender beliefs; religious and cultural beliefs, the list is long. And if left unchallenged, each one can have a strongly damaging effect on our abundance-consciousness.

Our prayer is that by using the elicitations and clear-out work in this book, you will uncover the myriad forms of beliefs that have undermined you for years – that you will uncover all the flavours of beliefs that are yours – and that you will so completely clear them out that their subversive legacy will stop right here, with you.

Cultural Beliefs

Some disempowering and limiting beliefs can become so solidly engrained that an entire culture agrees en masse that they are actually ironclad *facts*, the *truth* about 'the way life is'. Then no one bothers to investigate their efficacy, or questions whether there is any truth at all to them. It is tacitly accepted and agreed: "This is the way of life, and it will never change". Our negative beliefs have turned into concrete convictions.

These collective beliefs can encase or imprison entire cultures. On the surface they may seem immoveable, unshakeable, impenetrable, but we have discovered that through Journeywork even beliefs that have been passed down for hundreds of generations can be liberated, and wholeness-consciousness can take their place.

In recent years, The Journey has become greatly loved in Israel, and several rabbis approached our offices in Europe asking us to bring this healing work to their war-torn country. The general thirst for the work was so great, the desire for healing so strong, that we responded to the urgent call by immediately offering a foundational seminar with a Journey presenter. A few months later I followed that by personally giving a Journey Intensive.

At that first Intensive, many people unearthed traumatic cell memories that were a reflection of a jointly held consciousness: the Jewish people had thousands of years' history to confirm that they would always suffer war, pain, loss and persecution. The most solidly held belief was that the Jews had always and would always be persecuted, and this persecution-consciousness drove one conviction that nearly everyone agreed upon: "We never forgive, and never forget".

But in spite of their heritage, there was a huge prayer for healing, for forgiveness, for wholeness, and during that first seminar my heart was rawly splayed open by their willingness to welcome and face their darkest demons, their most horrific cell memories, and their fiercest pain in order to find peace in the core of their suffering.

Following these first events, fifteen Jewish Journey grads went to Sderot, a town on the border of Gaza which has been bombed almost daily for the last six years, and offered the process work to Arabs who lived there. Most of the volunteers had themselves experienced only two Journey processes, but they reached out to those who had suffered the trauma of continuous missile attacks for months, even though there was a real risk to their own lives. Their love, humility and courage blew me away. In spite of the very real dangers and the resistances they faced, they brought compassion and healing to an area that deeply needed it.

At the Abundance retreat that followed, our Journey presenter, Debs, was guiding a woman in her late sixties through the campfire section of an Abundance Journey process, in a live demonstration on stage. The cell memory that spontaneously arose was vivid and intense, as if it were occurring in that moment. It related to WWII and the murder of many of her family members in Germany by Nazis. At this campfire more than sixty years later, she was finally given the chance to release all the rage, hatred, despair and devastation about the Holocaust. When Adolf Hitler showed up in her process, six decades' worth of suppressed, unspoken, unexpressed pain came tearing out of her. When she had completely let go of what seemed like lifetimes of anguish and tears, the almost unthinkable happened. In front of a room filled with mainly Jewish people, though everyone recognised that the actions of Hitler and the Nazis were a horror that could never be condoned or forgiven, somehow, through the largeness of her being she found it in her heart to forgive the soul of Hitler. Her forgiveness of his soul by her soul was so real, so full, so radically healing that she finally came to peace with a painful consciousness that had been with her for well over 60 years.

The cultural dam broke. Everyone in the room fell apart emotionally. It seemed that thousands of years of persecution-consciousness was finally given permission to come up and out of people's hearts. It came pouring out from their deepest recesses.

Later, when everyone went into their own personal Abundance Journey processes, most of them welcomed to their campfires some aspect of the beliefs that had shackled their culture – and they released the consciousness of persecution that had been with them from birth. It was humbling beyond words to consider that this level of healing was possible.

Thirty-eight of the participants from that retreat decided to continue with the full European Practitioners' Programme, and their next module was the weeklong No Ego retreat that was taking place in a state-of-the-art carbon neutral eco hotel in the heart of the countryside, in what was previously East Germany. The hotel also happened to be situated a short distance away from the site of a former Nazi concentration camp.

For many Israelis, it was a huge stretch. For some it meant returning to their country of forbears' birth, stepping onto ancestral soil for the first time. All of them would be gathering at a place that was just 30 miles from a site laden with Holocaust significance.

But their joint prayer for forgiveness was greater than their fear of facing the worst of their cell memories, and like heroes they rallied together and arrived in Germany in time to celebrate the Sabbath, before the seminar began. One participant who had never travelled outside of Israel had been instructed by her Rabbi: "Go to Germany and learn how to forgive and heal. Then come back home to Israel and teach us all how to forgive." And it seemed they all embodied that profound healing intention.

There was much excitement, anticipation and not a little fear reverberating through the atmosphere on that first evening of the programme. People from countries all over Europe and beyond had congregated in this location. As well as from Israel, they came from Holland, England, Ireland, Wales, France, Italy, Germany, Austria, Switzerland, Croatia, Russia, Estonia, Finland, Sweden, and from farther afield: Dubai, Kenya, Japan, Australia, Peru, The Caribbean, South America and the U.S. It was a cultural melting pot with 18 nationalities cosseted together in one room, and that first night felt charged with electricity.

The German-speaking nations were the largest single group, and they were sitting with their translation headsets on, at the left-hand side of the room. The Israelis, with their headphones, were together at the other side of the room. There was such a strong prayer for healing, for oneness, it was palpably shimmering in the air, as if both sides were trying to reach out to the other side, but somehow no one seemed to know how to bridge the cultural gap that was so viscerally apparent.

During a sharing session on the second night, I decided it was time to address the 'elephant in the room', the issue that everyone had been avoiding since we arrived, but no-one was openly acknowledging: the omnipresent issue of World War II.

So I invited the group to join me in a healing process in which we would welcome into our awareness any war-consciousness that might have been passed down either generationally or culturally. I shared with everyone that the vast majority of those of us in the room were born post-World War II, and had in fact no direct experience of the conflict, yet we still carried the guilt, shame, suffering and pain of previous generations. I suggested that WWII was not the only war-consciousness we all carry; that in fact almost *every* country has for centuries engaged in war, and that at various points in time each of our countries has played both victim and aggressor. No country, no people, no religion was exempt. War-consciousness has been passed down since the beginning of time; all of us carry it in our DNA, and our outer world, the macrocosm, is merely a reflection of our inner world, the microcosm.

The truth is we are constantly waging war within ourselves, against ourselves. We have so much anger, judgment, shame, blame, self-loathing and hostility against our own selves, against life, against even our loved ones that until this consciousness is cleared from our cells there will always be wars in our external world. We have waged ceaseless battles, closing our hearts to those who needed our help, cutting those we care about down to size with cruel judgement and criticism, steeling ourselves against life and turning our back on the truth when we got scared. Though we may not have had real guns, all of us have fired invisible bullets that have left internal scars, some of which seem never to go away. I told everyone that for true change to happen in our world, it would first have to start within each of us. Our shift in consciousness would be a living transmission of a new wholeness-consciousness capable of catalysing a shift in awareness in the whole world; but for that transformation to take place it would have to come first from within ourselves.

So I welcomed everyone to imagine a campfire, and to invite a younger version of our self to the fire. Leading them by example from the stage, I gently coaxed everyone to be nakedly real, to empty out all the ways in which we have been self-judgmental, hateful, and even cruel to ourselves. We sat with eyes closed, yet emotionally exposed as I encouraged everyone to release all the words of hostility, self-criticism and self-blame that had been crushing us, and to empty out the guilt that was weighing us down. I asked them to empty out the times we had cut someone down, to be real about the way we had hurt others, to empty out the ways we had forsaken God, and we spoke out loud those things we had done and said that we were not proud of, ashamed of, and we welcomed all the different aspects of war consciousness stored inside us. This was an intimate but lengthy clearing out. It was very raw.

Then I asked everyone to invite their ancestors to their campfire, and to let their forebears know that they would no longer perpetuate the suffering of war-consciousness they had inherited from them. I asked them to thank their ancestors for all the healthy beliefs that they might have been blessed with, but to finally let the unhealthy consciousness go.

Then we invited a mentor to completely sweep us clean from all of the passed-on negative beliefs, and to sever any energetic ties to our parents' unhealthy beliefs. As we severed that energetic cord we sent love down one end toward our relatives and let love return to embrace them. Then we watched as this healthy consciousness travelled back through the generations from child to parent to grandparent, right back to the beginning of time.

I asked everyone to let their ancestors know that the legacy of war consciousness stopped right here, right now.

Then they brought future generations to the campfire and envisioned passing on solely oneness-consciousness, devoid of any previous generation's war-consciousness.

Finally, everyone was ready for forgiveness, and everyone wholeheartedly forgave their parents for passing on this old painful consciousness. Forgiveness came pouring out of all our hearts, flooding the room. The entire seminar hall was awash with floods of tears, releasing, letting go and complete forgiveness of self, of others, of ancestors, of life, and even of God.

When we opened our eyes, I asked each person to turn to the person next to them and say, "I forgive you for the war-consciousness you previously harboured. And I ask for forgiveness for what I have carried."

In raw exposure, people looked into each other's eyes and spoke these simple words straight from their hearts. Then I invited them to find someone else in the room and to repeat the same words, "I forgive you for the war consciousness..."

Suddenly, the room erupted into a roiling sea of motion. People sobbed, hugged, forgave, and I watched as the Israelis started running toward the Germans, and the Germans ran with open arms to meet them. The forgiveness came rolling out in waves. Two hundred and eighty people were speechless, in tears. Dutch forgave Germans; Germans forgave Russians; French forgave Italians; Japanese forgave Americans; Israelis forgave Germans; Asians forgave Caucasians; Christians, Hindus, Muslims and Jews forgave each other. Everyone forgave everyone.

Soon there were no cultural, religious or racial boundaries anywhere. There were no barriers anywhere between anyone. All separation had fallen away and the whole room was awash in oneness. We were swimming in mutual forgiveness, in the simple knowledge that each of us had lived a human existence, and all walls had dissolved into this sea of love.

In clearing our war-consciousness we paved the way for others to do the same. We all realised the significance of this: if it can happen between peoples with a heritage of this much deep-seated enmity, it means it is possible for our world. We may have been only two hundred and eighty people, but if we were capable of forgiving and healing to this extent it means that humanity, our entire planet is capable of that same level of forgiveness and healing.

The Journey has offered programmes with forgiveness-based process work for indigenous communities around the world: with the Aboriginals in Australia; the Maoris in New Zealand; the Sami in northern Finland; the indigenous peoples of Africa; the First Nations tribes of North America. And the depth and completeness of forgiveness we have witnessed has been a common theme in all cultures.

If First Nations people, Aboriginals, Maoris and native Africans can forgive their Caucasian invaders; if Israelis can forgive Arabs, and Arabs can forgive Jews; if Christians and Hindus can forgive Muslims, and Muslims can forgive Christians and Hindus; if black can forgive white; if the oppressed can forgive their aggressors, then that means there is true hope for our world.

All the thousands of souls who have cleared their issues and forgiven themselves have opened the door for you to do the same. This is your invitation to face your deepest fears, clear your most prejudicial beliefs. This is your call to forgive yourself. For in self-forgiveness all forgiveness is possible. And as you forgive yourself you give permission to the world to forgive itself.

Your oneness-consciousness will transmit that possibility to our planet. We all need to play our part. We all are capable of healing ourselves and, as we do, we offer that same healing possibility to our world. From true forgiveness world peace is possible. "Let there be peace on earth, and let it begin with you."

"Let there be Peace among all Beings of the Universe.

Let there be Peace, Let there be Peace, Let there be Peace.

Om, Shanti, Shanti, Shanti." ~ H W Poonja (Papaji)

CHAPTER 4

Manifesting and Living a Guided Life in Conscious Abundance

By now we have realised how important it is to take the lids off our hidden comfort zones. We've learned how powerful it is to get to the root cause of our silent saboteurs and clear out their related cell memories. We know that as we clear our blocks, veils and shutdowns more and more of our essential self is exposed and becomes available. And it is from this awakened presence that conscious action springs and holistic manifestation is born.

Now we are ready to learn how to *remain* wide open in this infinite field of possibilities to let it flow us into action, as part of the co-creative dance of wholesome manifestation. But before we begin this process, we first need to dispel an erroneous notion that most of us have held to be true.

In western societies there is a commonly held belief that has been passed down to us for generations, one that many of us have lived our *entire lives* believing. We have inherited the false notion that if only we <u>have</u> what we most long for – the perfect partner; perfect kids; the ideal job, house, clothes, and car; the latest equipment and gadgets; the right amount of financial wealth – then we will be able to <u>do</u> what we always longed to do – spend romantic times with partner; play lovingly with our kids; take exciting vacations in exotic places; take more leisure time; compete successfully at sports; work more productively in our jobs; eat in the finest restaurants; go to the best parties; mix with the right sort of people – and then we will finally be able to <u>be</u> the way we always longed to be – successful, confident, secure, enriched, fulfilled, happy, at peace, complete; our real self.

It seems that we have agreed en masse on the premise that by *having* those things 'out there' we will be enabled to *do* what we always wanted to do, and we will then become fulfilled and expressed, finally able to *be* all that we are capable of being.

It is as if we have all been programmed that life's external trappings will give us our sense of self. So our life's focus has been on things that seem always to be just out of our reach, and this constantly reminds us that we are falling short. We are left dissatisfied with our lives, craving a deeper fulfilment that we seem never to experience. And we end up resenting life, blaming it for preventing us from feeling fully expressed, never finding the sense of self-worth that our acquisitions were meant to give us.

Since the advent of television, our acquisition-consciousness has spiralled out of control. In an effort to get us to buy their products, TV advertisers have idealised the ownership of material possessions. We are constantly bombarded with glossy images, stereotyped icons of what 'real' success looks like: expensive designer clothes; state-of-the-art appliances and computers; prestige German cars; impossibly perfect designer bodies sculpted by ingenious plastic surgeons; perfect smiles constructed by expensive orthodontists; uber-chic mansions affordable only by those who earn ten times our salary, on and on. The gap between the way we are *currently* living and how we believe we are *expected* to live has often widened to a point of absurd inaccessibility, and this expectation gap has only heightened our neurotic obsession.

We all *want* to feel good about ourselves. We want to feel happy and fulfilled, yet our media – TV and radio commercials; magazines; billboards; books; newspapers, in fact, most modern advertising – has programmed us to believe that our only route to that fulfilment is to *acquire* the lifestyle it propagates.

In our obsession to have the lifestyle that seems otherwise to be out of our reach, many of us have gone into massive debt. But such debt and the stresses it causes merely serves to compound our unhappiness and, as it feeds our addictive patterns, it sinks us deeper into despair. For our yearning is never quenched, and our neurotic behaviour simply confirms what we fear most about ourselves: that we do not have what it takes; that we are losers, incapable of creating and holding on to the true and lasting abundance we long for. Then we have closed the loop in our cycle of failure-consciousness, and we continue striving in vain to fill the hole inside with more and more 'things'.

The truth is that nothing we can attain can give us the sense of self-worth and lasting fulfilment we are seeking. We will always want more, new and different – and it will *never* be enough. The notion that by *having* we will get to *do* what we want and *be* who we really are is one of the greatest lies humankind has sold itself. It is an utter fallacy!

The truth about *wholesome* abundance is that it actually happens *the other way around*. Instead of the old paradigm of having → doing → being, true manifestation occurs in the opposite direction, through being → doing → having.

When you have cleared the blocks that obscure your true potential and are wide open in a field of all possibilities, this awakened presence will naturally and effortlessly flow you into conscious action, and that in turn will lead you to the healthy manifestation of the material things in life. When you are wide open *as* pure *beingness* it automatically propels you into healthy, conscious action – *doingness* – and the natural result is *havingness*.

So, our having is simply a by-product of our being and doing. Yet, even when expensive material objects and vast wealth manifest in our lives, it is important to remember that this is merely the play-dough of reality. And play-dough will always be play-dough: it cannot provide us with true or lasting fulfilment, it cannot give us our own self. To believe that it can is a prescription for deep disappointment, devastating disillusionment.

Have you ever wondered why some celebrities who on the surface appear to have everything – fame; fortune; prestige; cars; mansions; travel – end up with severe problems of addiction or even kill themselves? It is often because they too believed the fallacy that the trappings of material success would make them feel complete, whole and at peace. And they often invested all of themselves – huge amounts of time and energy – in their quest to attain the life of their dreams, to 'have it all'. But when all the *having* occurred, even though they got to *do* what they wanted, it still did not give them what they were truly seeking: a sense of essential *beingness* – self-worth; self-acceptance; self-love; true greatness. They realised that *all* their attempts to find something meaningful and permanent had been futile. Their dream was shattered, and it left them hollow and empty, acutely disillusioned. At the end, in the depth of their disintegrated despair, they saw no way 'home' and they turned to drugs or suicide as the only ways out.

Believing that the trappings of success, in fact, believing that *anything* outside of you will bring you ultimate fulfilment is a dangerous game to play. It is a guaranteed recipe for unhappiness, one that will totally disempower you, leave you utterly empty-handed, devoid of the essential *beingness* you were really seeking.

When you were a kid, did you ever have the experience of your parents buying a new family car? Do you remember what that felt like – with everyone gathered around it, remarking on its style, its comfort, praising its great qualities? And do you recall how satisfying that *kerchunk* sound was when you first shut the doors, and how special it felt to take your first drive with the family? For a short while it was truly exhilarating, genuinely exciting.

But do you remember what it was like a week or two later, when you came home from school and walked straight past the car in the driveway, barely noticing it, not giving it a second glance, as if it were just a hunk of inert metal? It is because that initial flush of fulfilment could never last, and some part of your being had already figured out that the car could not really *give* you anything of value. It was just another object among many objects that come and go in life.

~

I had been touring around France in our luxury RV, on vacation with my wife and our eighteen-month-old son. We had arrived in Cannes, and were walking along the sea front in the early evening. I was feeling restless.

Although I had achieved an amount of success by my mid-thirties – a beautiful wife; an adorable son; a five-bedroom oceanfront house; a Porsche sports car; wonderful vacations – I was not 'there' yet. I had noticed that with material success came bigger dreams, and that as soon as one longed-for goal was achieved, my focus automatically shifted to something bigger and better.

At home I owned a great little sports boat, and we had a lot of fun and excitement with friends and family waterskiing, playing on the local lakes and coastline bays. But I wanted more; I wanted a bigger boat, an oceangoing motor yacht – something more prestigious, more impressive. I had learned how to goal set, and had written down exactly what that yacht would be: a 60-foot Sunseeker, in navy blue and white.

As I stood there in Cannes, gazing out over the Mediterranean, I saw the *exact* yacht of my dreams anchored close by: same model, same colours. Its owners and their chicly dressed friends sat on the rear deck, laughing as they drank cocktails.

"Wow!" I thought. "That's it. That's the one. When I have one of *those* I'll *know* I've made it. Life will be ideal."

As the thoughts arose, something strange happened: I had a satori moment. It felt as if I was somehow energetically transported *onto* the yacht – not like I was just mentally imagining it, but as if I was viscerally and emotionally engaged in the experience, as if it were actually happening. And *I* was drinking cocktails on *my* yacht with *my* friends and *my* family.

In that moment a terrible realisation washed through me: I *still* felt unfulfilled, separate. I still felt that something was missing from my life. I was still restless and essentially unhappy. I felt sick in my guts as the truth became clear: no matter what I achieved, no matter what expensive symbols of success I acquired, none of it would ever give me what I truly needed to make me feel authentically and permanently good about myself.

The belief system that I had most identified with in life – that I would achieve significant financial success and that that success would be the panacea for everything that was wrong with me and my life – was entirely shattered. It was as if all my hopes for a better, brighter future had been sucked out of me, and I felt devastated.

The experience caused me to reappraise every aspect of my life: my career; my marriage; my whole lifestyle. It ultimately drove me to begin a different type of search; a search for something deeper, something genuinely meaningful. I spent two frantic years *seeking* the truth: attending many seminars, scouring spiritual and esoteric books, and listening to hundreds of audiotapes desperately *trying to find* what was missing in my life.

Then, by accident it seemed, I discovered The Journey. I booked a one-to-one session, though I didn't know what it entailed. What unfolded during that two-hour session was the most deep-seated transformation of my entire life.

I had experienced many modalities of personal growth and healing over the years, but this was astonishingly different. With little preamble I was asked to stop, tune into my body and identify what I was feeling emotionally. It was anxiety, fear. Then, instead of manipulating or analysing what I was feeling, instead of trying to find a way to make it feel better, I was simply told to *welcome* the emotion – all of it. Soon I was opening into layers of emotions, each one deeper, more poignant than the last. Eventually, I felt that I had reached the end: beneath the worthlessness, isolation and despair, I arrived at death's door. It seemed like I was going to die. I let go, surrendered completely, and it felt like some physical dissolution took place. When it stopped I silently inquired, "What's here? What is this?" It was pure awareness, shimmering, alive. As I relaxed it opened wider, it became vast, infinite, and permeated with light. I fell into a peace so deep that nothing could disturb it, a bliss so pervasive that nothing could alter it. I had come home. This was the enlightened presence I had, without knowing it, been seeking all my life. This was my own essence. There was nothing more to find. My search was over.

I had grown up believing that success and achievement would define me, and would bring me fundamental satisfaction and happiness. I had believed that some display of that achievement would serve to quiet the doubting, critical voices of others that still played in my mind, and that my own fears and insecurities would be quelled, and that ultimately I would find real self-worth and peace. But each belief was seen to be a lie, absolutely busted. Though the acquisition of desirable material goods had often brought with it a rush of wellbeing, it was only ever a temporary change of state. And though it had often been fun and adventurous to play with the acquired toys, those feelings too were fleeting. None of it had ever *permanently* altered my core inner state, and I realised now that nothing outside me could *ever* do that. Nothing outside me could ever give me anything lasting.

Hand-in-hand with this debunking of old beliefs came an extraordinary realisation: everything I had ever searched for is *already* within me, and it is effortlessly accessible at all times.

I discovered within myself an innate truth, and I knew this truth to be permanent. It was not as if anything had been gained, nothing had been attained nor added into me: what I uncovered had always been this full, this complete – and nothing, no one, could take that discovery away.

My ongoing life experience was enriched beyond measure. It became more vibrant, more colourful, more fulfilled. And though I became more engaged in everyday life, more authentically and fully a part of it, life's dramas – and there were several – could not touch, could not undermine the essence of me. I lived in pure bliss, deep peace, for the next *five months*, until eventually I felt hooked by an emotional issue, and I used the same Journey process to clear it. I then opened freshly, even more deeply into freedom and, ever since, this freedom has been the undercurrent to my life, it is the *context* in which my life occurs.

This that I am is *already* complete, is *inherently* whole, needs nothing to fulfil it. Abundance already pervades all of life, and *I am that*.

~

The bottom line is this: nothing external can ever complete you. Nothing external can ever give you who you really are.

So in this book we will discard our old painfully destructive notions, and instead choose to learn how to manifest abundance consciously, healthfully, from a place of inherent fulfilment – from a wholeness that has *already* been realised. This awakened presence naturally flows us into healthy action, which leads to the conscious co-creation of abundance. We will learn how to be part of the dance of manifestation, all the while fully realising it cannot give us anything other than the joy of co-creation, and that the fruits of that co-creation cannot give us the fulfilment of our self.

The amazing thing is that, once you have awakened to the true greatness within you, once you have opened into the boundless potential that is your own essence, what you discover is something *no one* can take from you. It is something that cannot be *un*learned. It is something you recognise as being intrinsic, timeless and eternal; it is not something that can disappear. No manifestation of wealth or material belongings can add anything to it; it is already full and complete. In knowing who you are, being a part of the process of manifestation becomes a gift, a privilege. You recognise the immense blessing in being able to play your part in facilitating conscious abundance. Yet ultimately, as joyous as this dance becomes, as naturally grace-filled as it is, the magic of it cannot make you whole or complete – it cannot make you any *more* of what you already are.

In this chapter we will learn how to let the grace of our being guide us into the fulfilment of our own destiny. We will learn *how* to be part of the co-creative dance of conscious manifestation, *how* to live a guided graceful life.

The Principles of Manifestation

How to Live a Guided Life in Conscious Abundance

Before we plunge into the Principles of Manifestation, we would like to offer a caveat. We want to be crystal clear that we are not suggesting that we have found the key that unlocks the whole mystery of the universe. We are not suggesting that we have figured out *how* the mystery of creation works, nor are we saying that this is *the secret* or that these are *the divine laws* of manifestation. To do so would be supremely arrogant. The mystery of creation is essentially that – a mystery. It is vast, wonderful, magical, unfathomable and unknowable. And the truth is that we are personally content to *live* in the mystery, to be part of it, and to play our part in the dance. We do not believe we will ever plumb the depths of this mystery, nor fully comprehend the nature of the universe. In fact, we do not believe *anyone* will ever *fully* understand it.

Instead, what we offer here are suggestions, guidelines that have proven powerfully effective in the process of participating in manifesting conscious abundance. Life is the most powerful and extraordinary teacher we know, so all we can share with you are some potent principles that have been revealed to us through direct experience, and which when applied have proven to get healthy, lasting results. *How* it all occurs is up to the universe.

There has been such grace-filled, bountiful and healthy manifestation around The Journey ever since its first inception fifteen years ago. Far more has occurred than we could have possibly conceived. And over time we have come to experience that as more and more of our own lids and veils have fallen away, more of our own essence, the infinite field has been exposed. And more of this unborn potential has become available to be used by life in this ongoing play of creation.

As more freedom has shown up in our lives, it is as if the universe 'got it' that there was a greater capacity available for us to be used as vehicles in the process of co-creation. We have been automatically propelled into effortless action, and more and more manifestation has occurred naturally, of its own accord.

Let Grace be in Charge

In our lives there has been deep surrender and a simple, unquestioning trust in life – that it knows what it is doing, and *why* – and even though its mechanics and underlying reasons may forever remain a mystery, there has been an increasing ease in allowing grace to fully take the helm. It has become clear that there is a higher purpose in the divine's plan, and that whenever we surrender and trust that what is happening is what is *meant* to happen, that openness allows us to respond to the wordless guidance that is always available from our essence. Direction, answers, inspiration are *always* here, always available.

This is why the greater portion of this book has been focused on clearing the silent saboteurs, beliefs and lids. As they fall away, you *naturally* open, and can listen more deeply to life, feel and respond effortlessly to the intrinsic guidance that is always available. This guidedness will flow you into action that will organically lead you to the manifestation your soul has put out for.

The Power of Healthy, Unobstructed Positive Intention

At the beginning of Chapter Two we mentioned the power of unobstructed, healthy, positive intentions to catalyse manifestation into form. In fact, modern physics has demonstrated that when you focus on a desired positive outcome with the intent to take purposeful action to achieve the results, your chances of manifesting what you want are hundreds of thousands of times greater than if you had just a random thought float through your awareness. Science has shown that purposeful intent is a powerful force for causing the unmanifest to manifest, to express itself in physical form.

We also mentioned that, even though intentions are a powerful force for manifestation, they are only successful in achieving the desired results if there are no mitigating unconscious negative intentions simultaneously going out. These negative intentions can have a neutralising effect on the positive ones, no matter how strongly we might try to use our will to override them. Only by clearing your unconscious negative impulses, the silent saboteurs and negative beliefs, can your positive intentions be unhindered on their way to fruition.

So it is time to begin learning how we can proactively participate in this wondrous journey of manifesting abundance. Here are the hows:

Do the Clearing Process Work *First*

In our Manifest Abundance retreat a comprehensive sweep-clean prefaces all our Journeys in Manifestation. We always begin by undergoing the full, unabridged, Abundance Journey process – the one included in the last section of this book. We also do the Fear Process, and Beliefs Change Process. Then from unbounded potential, we open and offer ourselves to be guided.

The Magnetising Power of Gratitude and the Repelling Force of Neediness

It is said that gratitude is a natural magnet for grace, and it is our direct experience that "More is added unto the one with a grateful heart". When your cup is overflowing with gratitude for all the blessings that life has already showered you with, life cannot resist you. It feels compelled to grace you with *more* of what you are grateful for.

Have you ever listened to an ungrateful friend, someone who appears quite blessed, but still moans incessantly that there is never enough? They may complain that their partner is not around enough, their high-paying job is not really satisfying, their body is not slim enough, their vacation was not long enough... on and on, they just keep griping about everything being *less* than it should be. They live with a cup that is eternally half empty, and spend their lives bitterly complaining about their lot. Have you ever noticed your internal response to all this ingratitude and complaint – that you felt drained, uninspired, flat, and ultimately a bit repelled?

And have you ever had the opposite take place; where a friend of yours who seems to live modestly, humbly, has shared with you how lucky they feel, how blessed they are to have such a wonderful partner, what a gift it is to have a job that pays the bills, how fortunate they feel to have such amazing kids and how privileged they feel to have a place they can call home? They effuse about how lucky they are in life; their cup overflows with genuine thankfulness. What was your internal response? Did you find that you were moved by that person, touched, perhaps even graced by their innocent gratitude? And did you find yourself hoping that somehow life would add unto their good fortune, feeling they really *deserved* to have all the blessings that life could bestow on them, and knowing that they would truly honour and appreciate what ever might come their way?

It is true: no one can resist a thankful heart, an appreciative soul. It is a natural magnet that attracts blessings. And so it is with grace: it cannot resist gratitude; it is inextricably drawn to a grateful heart.

There is a second benefit to opening up to all you are grateful for in life. When your heart is overflowing with thankfulness, when there is deep appreciation of how blessed, how fortunate you are, have you ever noticed how complete you feel? Nothing is required, nothing wanted. Your heart feels at peace, even your ego is at rest, no longer grasping for things. When the heart is brimming over, nothing is needed, nothing more is required; you are already complete, already whole.

Gratitude is a healthy place from which to begin our Journey in Manifestation.

Desperate Neediness Pushes Abundance Away

Our experience is that any time you feel you absolutely *must* have something, that you desperately need it, your need will push what you long for further and further away. Desperate need has a polarising, repelling effect on manifestation.

Have you ever been in relationship with someone who desperately needed you, who required your sole attention day and night, constantly craving your love, affection, and praises? What was your genuine response? Did you feel naturally drawn to shower them with the more compliments, kind words and encouragement, thereby feeding the need? Or, after a time, were you a little repelled? Did you eventually find yourself recoiling from their desperation, even backing off from it, maybe even feeling slightly repulsed and eventually seeking some way to extricate yourself from the relationship? If we are honest, most of us feel turned off by neediness. It has a repelling force that pushes away the very thing it is craving.

Desperate neediness communicates to life that we do not trust it to take care of us; that we do not believe life will grace us in abundance; that we will forever be unheard, unseen and unblessed. And we tend to manifest what we believe. While we are trying to force life to fulfil our cravings, demanding it fills our needs, what we are longing for is pushed further and further away from us, and eventually eludes us entirely. In fact, the most effective way to ensure that you *do not* get something is to *demand* you get it, *insist* it is given to you. Life is *not a universal ordering system*, and you can pretty much guarantee that if you treat it as such, your ego-needs will drive genuinely healthy abundance out of your life.

However, when you are swimming in an ocean of gratitude, overwhelmed by the blessedness of life, anything is possible. With an attitude of gratitude, you become a magnet for grace. And it is from here that healthy intentions can go out.

Writing Down What You Are Grateful For

Start your Journey in Manifestation by writing down all you are grateful for in life, to remind yourself how blessed you are and to make those blessings more tangible, more real. Take out a journal and write at the top of the first page: "What am I most grateful for in life? How have I been blessed, and what have these gifts given me emotionally?" Then close your eyes and welcome into your awareness all the blessings, the material things, people, and gifts that have graced you in life. Be specific, and contemplate the various relationships you have; how lucky you are to have a job; how blessed you are to have a roof over your head, healthy food to eat, clothing to wear. Welcome all the skills you have developed, the talents you have been gifted with, the realisations and understandings you have uncovered. Add in the vacations you have taken, the friendships you enjoy, the nourishing nature walks you have taken, and so on. Let the abundance that is present in your life flood your awareness and then open your eyes and let it pour onto the page. Become a scribe for abundance and, like automatic writing, allow all your blessings to get listed in your journal. Include the simple things in life; the joy that children's laughter brings; the excitement of a great movie or a sports match; the smell of beautiful flowers; the inspiration your favourite music gives you; the cosiness of a fireside chat, or the excitement of a board-game played with your loved ones. Keep filling the pages until your heart wants to burst with the magnitude of how lucky and privileged you are.

Once you are aware that your cup is overflowing, that you are immersed in a sea of abundance, go back through your list and ask about each item,

"What do these things give me emotionally? What emotional benefits do they bring?" This will bring a fullness, a richness to your appreciation of the abundance you have been blessed with in life.

When I do this I often end up in floods of tears as I let the magnificence, the wonder of it all overwhelm me. I am blown away by the immensity of abundance that is here, available each and every moment. I get lost in awe.

When I see my grandchildren's names written down on my list and I ask what emotional gift I receive from them, I realise they are a source of great joy and delight in my life. When I see my daughter's name on the page I realise how full I feel in my love for her. When Kevin's name appears I recognise how much I feel at home in his presence, I feel oneness, privileged to have a partner to share my vision with. When I contemplate my profession, I realise how lucky and deeply fulfilled I am that life has allowed me to follow my heart's calling and respond to grace's purpose in serving humanity. On and on, I recognise the depth of how blessed I am, and what emotional gains these blessings evoke for me. Asking this question gives the play-dough of life richness and dimension.

Once you have completed your list of blessings and emotional gains, and you feel your heart cannot hold another thing, you are ready to begin the next step in your Journey in Manifestation.

Using Self-inquiry to Open into the Ocean of Abundance

From overflowing fullness you can, with a simple, powerful question, begin to discover the nature of this infinite field of abundance. Close your eyes, settle in your being, and begin inquiring from within:

"Who am I in abundance?... Who am I?"

As you ask this question, stay still and open, and allow any answers to arise naturally from within. Be innocent and genuinely long to know who you really are in abundance. Let the divine, the deepest part of you give rise to the truth.

At first some labels might arise, "I'm a businessperson, a mother, a husband...", but eventually the labels will run out, and your own essence will start drawing you deeper into the infinite field, where you will recognise an unborn potential that is longing to give birth to creation. You will realise that this presence wants to use you to be part of that co-creative dance.

Keep opening into this wondrous, pure potential. Keep inquiring, "Who am I in abundance?" As you do, this field of abundance will reveal its multifaceted, limitless, omnipresent nature.

You are now ready for the next stage of your journey.

The Power of Writing Positive Intentions

Open your eyes and turn to a new page in your journal. Stay wide open in this exhilarating ocean of all possibilities, and write at the top of the page, "What does grace *most* want for me? What is the *highest vision* that life has for me? What is the *highest and best* that could take place?" Then close your eyes again and allow expansive abundance to flood your awareness with the answers to these questions. Grace always wants the highest and best, and it is always capable of achieving its own prayers and intentions. So, staying wide open to all possibilities, begin welcoming into your awareness the vision that life has in store for you. Look at every aspect of your life – your relationships; your career; your creativity; your health; your leisure activities; your contribution to life – and like an innocent child let the infinite fill your awareness with what it most wants in these areas of your life. Now open your eyes and, once again, let it all pour effortlessly onto the page.

The Power of the Written Word

There is a mysteriously powerful effect in writing down your positive intentions. During the late 1970s there ended a twenty-five-year study done on a specific class of Harvard graduates. When they were students, three percent of the grads had written down their goals and the actions they planned to take to achieve them. Ninety-seven percent of them had not. When the study was concluded it was discovered that the three percent who wrote down their goals were worth more in financial terms than all the other ninety-seven percent together!

There is some inexplicable but quantifiable power in *writing down* positive intentions. In the yogic scriptures they refer to this phenomenon as *matrika shakti*, the power of the written word. We have come to the conclusion that as long as these ideas just swim through awareness, they remain ephemeral; they have no concrete reality of their own. But once you write them down, you have given them their first form, their first expression in physical reality, and we believe this has a concretising effect on the intention; it makes it more focused, more solid, more real. So, instead of simply allowing a vision to come to you, write it down.

The Power of Non-personal Intention

As you have noticed, we did not ask you to write at the top of the page, "What do *I* most want in my life? What is *my* highest vision?" We asked you to write it in a non-personal way, as if you are merely a scribe, a vehicle for grace to download its positive intentions for your life. This eliminates any personal neediness from the process. You are already experiencing yourself to be a vast field of possibilities. You are full, whole and as such your ego requires nothing, so when you write, "What does grace most want for me?" it allows your thinking mind, your ego, to stay out of the way, it allows true inspiration to find its way onto the page with no personal objections or needs getting in the way. It also eliminates any tendency you might have for censoring some part of the vision.

No Censorship

As a non-personal scribe for this inspiration you must stay out of censorship. Sometimes the mind can check in, and the ego will try to persuade you that these intentions are too grand, too lofty, unachievable – maybe even that it is not what the 'I' actually desires. If this happens, simply stop, breathe and welcome your ego-mind to fall into the background, and just ask once again, "Who am I in abundance?" The question will carry you directly back into your boundless essence, and once again you can continue as an empty scribe. Ask yourself, "What is the highest and best that *life* wants for me in this area?" Then open and let it fall onto the page.

Be Specific

Once the entire vision has been downloaded, go back over what you have written. What has been created is essentially a general broad-stroke description of what grace wants to manifest in your life. Find the juicy bits, the parts of the vision that really inspire you, and *get specific*, really flesh them out. You can even write several pages, a mini novelette, about one specific intention.

It is absolutely *essential* to get specific and detailed in the intention. Otherwise life will not know exactly what is wanted and you will waste a lot of precious time looking at things that are not *really* what was envisioned. When you get completely clear it is much more likely that grace will manifest your vision in a reasonable amount of time; and you will be much more likely to *recognise* it when it arrives.

If a four-bedroom house is envisioned, life will need to know specifically what kind of house is needed. In order for life to lead you to it, you need to be crystal clear, very detailed, very thorough. The truth is there are a millions of four-bedroom houses in the world, but probably only a small handful will meet your real requirements.

What do you want the rooms to look like? How big are they? What size are the windows? What view do you want to see from them? What size property is the house on? What does the yard look like? What area is the house in? If you have children, what kind of school district do you wish to be in? How else do you want the neighbourhood to feel? What sort of neighbours do you want? How far from work should it be? How do *you and your family* want to *feel* when you are at home? How do you want *others* to feel when they visit you? What is your maximum conscious budget? When is your move-in date? On and on, as you get more specific you add a lot of energy and focus to the vision, and this allows you to feel very clear when you are actively out there locating it.

Complete the Full *Vision Quest*

Once you have gone through a thorough descriptive envisioning of all the intentions grace has for your life, you need to complete the rest of your intentioning, your *Vision Questing* process. Up until now you have written down only what you would like to *attract* or *magnetise* to your life. Now you need to complete the full manifestation picture by writing out how you want to *maintain, grow* and *flourish* the abundance that you have manifested, and then work out how you are going to *let abundance flow back out to life*. You need to complete the cycle.

Maintaining, Flourishing and Growing Abundance

So at the top of a new page write, "How do I want to maintain, grow and flourish abundance?" Then repeat through the entire envisioning process you did before, letting the answers in this area flow like automatic writing onto the page. If you have magnetised a car into your life, how will you maintain it and care for it? If you have attracted a new partner, how will you grow and flourish the relationship? If you get a new job, how will you grow and develop in your career? If new skills have been acquired, how will you hone and practice them? If children have graced your life, how will you nurture and guide them so they can flourish? How will you invest in yourself and your own self-development?

Let all the ways you will honour, cherish and grow the abundance in your life fall onto the page. Make it as real and thorough as possible. It makes the vision come alive it gives your intentions real energy. And remember to add into your list how each of these choices makes you *feel emotionally*.

Letting Abundance Flow Back Out to Life

Once you have thoroughly written down how you will flourish and grow the abundance in your life, it is time to complete the cycle by inquiring how you will allow it to flow gracefully back out to life. Ask how you can contribute abundance back to life. Can your home be shared, used as a getaway by a friend or family member when you are not there? Could you give a neighbour a ride to work? Maybe there are others who could benefit from using your car when you are not using it? Perhaps you have skills that you could pass on to others: coaching a youth sports team, or mentoring a junior at work, maybe. If you have a talent you might like to offer that gift by donating a painting, or singing, or dancing for a charitable organisation. If you have healing skills, or reading and writing skills, or technology skills, you could offer coaching to someone who cannot afford it. Maybe you could offer a meditation evening or a personal development session to your friends. When you bake a pie, bake two, and give one away to a neighbour. When you watch a film, invite a friend to watch it with you. Go through your closet regularly and give away any clothes you do not absolutely love or are not using. If you are going on holiday, take a relative or friend with you. There are *so* many ways to give back the abundance in which you have been showered.

So write on the top of a new page "How do I want abundance to flow back out to life? How do I want to contribute? How do I want to share?" And then like a scribe for grace let it fall onto the page. And once again, make a note of how all this letting go and sharing of blessings makes you *feel emotionally*.

Everything in life is a gift that can be shared and when you allow grace to flow out to life, you will find it opens the door for more to flow *into* your life. Life is a never-ending cycle of abundance. And the more precise you are with your envisioning, the more likely it is to happen in the most delightfully unexpected and magical ways.

Add in Timelines

Next, go back through all your manifestation intentions and, remaining wide open in abundance-consciousness, write a time or a date next to each of the major prayers. Hold in you awareness that grace is saying, "In this time or quicker. By this date or sooner." This process further concretises the reality of your intentions, and lets life know that what you have described is not simply an open-ended wish list, but that it is a real vision with specific time frames.

Be Accurate and Precise

It is essential when you are writing out the intentions, that you are precisely accurate about the specifications and qualities required. Life is capable of manifesting whatever it scribes through you, and if you unintentionally leave out an essential or important element or part of your vision, you could end up manifesting *exactly* what you have written instead of the *complete* vision you *believed* was wanted.

In the early years of The Abundance Retreat I had not yet uncovered an important principle of manifestation, so I had not started cautioning people to be careful what they put out for. Once you are free, clear and wide open, the chances are your intentions will manifest *very* quickly, probably sooner than you think – so it pays to be extra careful!

Be Careful What You Put Out For

Ten years ago a bright, determined, ambitious twenty-three-year-old woman, fresh out of university, came to our Abundance Retreat in England. During one of the breaks, she wrote an extensive description of her intended dream job. Laurie had achieved top grades at college in business and marketing, and she wanted her first job to reflect what she perceived to be her up-to-the-minute expertise in the field. She was clear that, because of her great qualifications and recommendations, she did not want to start at the bottom rung of the corporate ladder. So she put out for a middle management position in a prestigious, up-market, advertising agency in west London, which was an easy commute for her. She preferred a boutique-type company instead of a faceless corporation, so that she wouldn't get lost in it. She got very specific, down to the exact salary she wanted, which was high considering she had just graduated from university.

Three weeks after the retreat, Laurie landed the *exact* job that she had described in her journal. It was identical, right down to the finest detail – prestige, boutique agency; middle-management position; precisely the right salary – it was even in Notting Hill, a trendy area in west London. She was thrilled that she had been so precise, and delighted she had got the perfect result – or so she thought!

Make Sure You Genuinely Want What You Put Out For

Laurie turned up for her first week at work and was horrified by her co-workers. She had forgotten to envision and describe how she wanted to *feel* at work, and the *kind of people* she wanted surrounding her. She was appalled at the political backstabbing, the lying, and the vicious gossip that she was subjected to from day one. But as this was her first bona-fide corporate stint, she felt she would damage her long-term career if she reneged on her first contract, so she ended up spending a nightmare year in a job she hated.

At the end of that year, Laurie came back to the Abundance Retreat, and she cleared more of her silent saboteurs. Once again she vision quested a new job. This time she was absolutely clear about *every* aspect of it. She wanted to use her marketing expertise to serve an organisation that had a mission to make a difference to humanity. She wanted to be surrounded by conscious, caring work colleagues, who had a personal calling to serve life, who had committed themselves to truth. She wanted to make a real difference for others in life.

Three-and-a-half weeks later, I felt a spontaneous pull to call Laurie. She had been such a bright star at the retreat – shiny, radiant, intelligent, awake – and someone had told me she lived in my area. So I asked her if she would like to go horse riding with me; she seemed athletic and I was looking for a riding partner. On our hack, I mentioned that The Journey was looking for someone who had a love of truth and a longing to serve humanity, who could help us get the word out about the work. We needed someone with enthusiasm and drive to work in our offices. She confided in me that we shared the same prayer and when she told me what her field of expertise was it seemed a perfect fit. Her making sure that she was accurate, precise and had painted a full picture allowed us to be magnetised to her, though we had no previous knowledge of her background. Laurie was with The Journey for eight years, and became a much-loved member of our team. She eventually became a director in our Australian company and headed up our office there until she left to start a family of her own.

Grace can manifest *anything*. Just be careful that you are fully complete and grounded in what you put out for, and that it is something you genuinely want.

Taking Action

After you have completed a detailed and meticulous vision and intention, you need to stay open to let it propel you into conscious action. You cannot just sit at home expecting abundance to come to you. You have to get out in the world and keep taking the effortless actions you are pulled to take. You must be willing to play an *active* part in fulfilling your intentions. We have a concrete belief that if the infinite is capable of creating a specific vision, it is also fully capable of manifesting it. This that *gave rise* to the prayer is the same presence that will *bring the fulfilment* of it. It is not your job to manifest *anything*. Your job is simply to stay wide open in an ocean of trust, letting it guide you to wherever in the world this abundance is *located*.

Do Not Second Guess Grace

I had staffed at dozens of Manifest Abundance retreats with Brandon, and at the end of each one of them I had taken the time to write down my intentions and offer up the biggest of them at a manifestation circle. And each time the prayer was similar, "Grace's prayer for me is to uncover and clear all the blocks and veils that obscure the truth of my own being. Life's highest prayer for me is to surrender completely and deepen in this freedom." Then in 1999, something unexpected happened, and it led to new lessons.

At one retreat I stood up to offer my intention in a manifestation circle, sure that what would be asked for was some version of my spiritual prayer. Instead, what I blurted out was, "Grace's highest vision for me in this moment is to manifest a new, bright yellow, Fiat sports car." Internally, I named the model and specification. I laughed out loud with embarrassment that my prayer, my offering in the circle, had been so blatantly material. The participants saw the joke and in a good-natured way laughed with me. "A yellow sports car! So that's the highest and deepest prayer in my life!" My laughter subsided and turned into a smile of recognition; grace was inviting me to lighten up and have fun – and would apparently make sure of it by manifesting a funky and racy Italian plaything.

I got still and opened to release the intention to the universe, and the group silently offered its support by seeing the prayer as already realised. It was hair-bristlingly powerful as the intention went out. I felt as if I was driving the car, like it was already mine. It seemed that the universe had done its job in that exact moment. All that was left was for me to do was to locate where in the world this car was.

The next week I started my search. Knowing that my budget was nearly twenty five percent less than the car's list price made me a little nervous about what responses I would get from dealers, and I forgot about the powerful sense I had had that the exact car had already been magnetised for me. I forgot to surrender and trust that I would be guided.

So I picked up the Yellow Pages, turned to the right section and, starting with the A's, began dialling the Fiat dealers in our general area. Most did not have the exact model I was looking for. Those that did either laughed or were derisive when I mentioned my budget. They assured me that what I was asking for was impossible – far less than they themselves would have paid for such a car. I laboured on in the same linear fashion, getting similar results at each number I called.

Do Not Second-Guess Yourself

I soon became disheartened, and began second-guessing myself. "What if I bought second hand?" I wondered. "What if it were blue, or red? In fact, what if I bought a different make altogether? Would that be more realistic? Would I be able to manifest that?"

For two weeks I changed tack. I made countless phone calls and dragged Brandon to showroom after showroom checking out numerous makes, models and colours of cars. Nothing worked: wrong performance or economy; uncomfortable seats; too little headroom; too unreliable according to the statistics; didn't like the looks – the faults of each car seemed like brick walls of unsuitability that blocked me from every angle. I got exasperated, and felt thwarted.

Brandon, eventually worn out by all my vacillation, asked, "Didn't you put out for a very specific *yellow Fiat* car at the Abundance Retreat a few weeks ago?"

"Yes", I replied, "I was very specific, and the intention seemed powerful at the time, but every dealer I spoke to almost choked when I mentioned my budget. I figure I must have made a mistake; life must have something else in store."

Trust Grace's Vision

"It's your efforting and your questioning that are the mistakes", she answered. "All your *pushing* is making you blind to the inevitable *pull* of grace. Once you've put out a clear and detailed intention you need to get out of the way, *let go*. Just know that grace has *already* manifested exactly what you are looking for, even if your mind has not yet caught up with the fact. All you need to do is to open and relax, and know that you'll be guided. Just trust."

I knew she was right. I recognised that my embarrassment around my modest budget had felt like I had champagne taste but only beer money. I had not surrendered or trusted; I had fallen back into an old pattern of trying to will something into becoming real. And I recognised that my old strategies were failing.

So I decided to stop second-guessing myself, and to relax and let go of my tight grip on the prayer that had gone out. I remembered that it was not my job to manifest anything, so I decided to open and trust. Within hours something felt different inside me. I no longer felt compelled or driven, and felt genuinely happy that the car would either appear or it would not. I sat back down at my desk and prepared to start some work, but something drew me back to the Yellow Pages, and it fell open to a section that was dog-eared from all my previous searching. Among all the Fiat dealers listed there my attention was drawn to only one. Whenever my eyes went to it my body relaxed and felt breezy about it. I called the number.

"Do you have in stock a new Broom Yellow Coupé, with the twenty-valve turbo engine, black leather interior and air conditioning?" I enquired.

"Hmm... yes", replied the salesman, "I believe we do."

"And would you be open to a deal on this car?" I asked. "I have no trade-in".

"I think we could work something out", he answered.

"Great! Then I'll be in to see you later this afternoon. What time do you close?"

Surrender and Trust

I went to the dealership and there was the car, with exactly my specifications. When I sat in the driver's seat I knew it: this was *the* car – this was the *exact* same feeling I had when I put out the original prayer at the retreat. And this time, when it came to discussing a discount, I felt comfortable and relaxed, almost confident. I simply asked the salesman to check what his best price could be, and with only a cursory amount of negotiation we agreed a price that was £400 *less* than the budget I had set. After letting go and trusting, it had taken only a few hours for grace to guide me to the perfect car at an incredible price. When I stopped wilfully pushing, my body was able to tune to the pull – and that pull led me directly to what grace had manifested some two weeks before.

The salesman explained: though the public announcement had not yet been made, Fiat head office in Italy had notified its dealers that a minor specification change would be made to this model starting next month. The new cars would be nearly ten percent more expensive, but my specification would no longer be the newest, latest (I didn't care!). When they saw the internal bulletin, the directors had decided to clear the old models by giving heavy discounts – that was just over *two weeks earlier*, at the time of the Abundance Retreat!

When grace writes from emptiness and births a prayer through you, forget all your old logical, linear approaches. Just let go, relax, open and trust. Let something *far* greater than your thinking mind take care of the rest.

Trust, Trust, Trust

When Gandhi was asked about a civil project, "Where are we going to get the money from?" he answered, "From wherever it is right now." He had a certain knowing that abundance is already here and available, and his only job was to locate it.

So we like to think of ourselves as friendly sharks in the ocean of trust. As soon as a vision has been specifically defined, a part of our awareness is constantly on the lookout; it is continually and effortlessly vigilant, staying wide open, waiting to be pulled, to be guided to wherever this thing is.

When Kevin and I first moved to Britain, we sat down and wrote out exactly what was required for an apartment west of London. We called a friend and asked if he would find us a two-bedroom apartment, in a semi-rural area within twenty miles of the city. We wanted something pristinely clean and professional. It needed to be light, open, and airy, with a big open-plan kitchen, dining room and living area. It should come furnished with modern, comfortable and clean furniture. We preferred high ceilings, and something newly remodelled would be perfect. It would be great to have a view of the River Thames, and it should be close to a train line so clients from London could get to our private practice easily. We gave him a rental budget and asked our friend to secure a three-month lease for us while we waited for our furniture to arrive from the States, after which we planned to get something more permanent. An apartment was found and our friend signed the lease on our behalf.

Kevin and I arrived at Heathrow airport and we drove straight to the property and met with the estate agent. It seemed like a perfect location, near transportation, a half-hour from London and directly overlooking the river. But the similarity to our vision ended at the front door. We entered a tiny, higgledy-piggledy postage stamp of a place spread over two floors, with miniature casement windows, and a tiny pilot kitchen. It had low ceilings and was dark. We thought we had been so clear, but the place was so unlike what we had wanted that it would have been entirely unprofessional to meet with our clients there.

Shocked at the dreariness of the flat, we were greatly relieved to find out that we could get out of the lease, and Kev and I drove to an airport hotel to regroup.

Never Compromise Grace's Vision

So we sat down again and became *even more* specific. We added into our vision that we wanted to have a place that was fresh, with none of the previous inhabitants' energy or family knick-knacks hanging around. We wanted more professional, executive style accommodation.

The next day, we struck out from our hotel and headed into Windsor, the nearest good-size attractive town that would have an estate agent. We were *very* clear in what we wanted, but every time we viewed a place, something about it was not quite right – too small; too far from the commuter trains; not green enough; the stale, leftover smell of its previous occupants or their dog – we went from house to house, apartment to apartment, and with each successive agent we tried to be clearer in the description of our needs. We did not want to waste time looking at places that were not right, that compromised what grace had written.

We have learned that if you compromise the vision that grace has written down – if you do not genuinely trust the universe to manifest *exactly* what it has been put out for – often the real thing that you were meant to find can pass you by, leaving you with something that doesn't feel right, that doesn't fit.

It was near the end of the day, and though we were getting clearer and clearer, the right place still had not yet presented itself. We pulled into the town of Ascot at 5:00 PM, and ran into the nearest estate agents. I quickly rattled off all the qualities we were looking for in a place and also launched into what we did not want. Finally the agent said, "Stop. I get what you want. You want a luxury executive apartment in some place green and convenient for transport. But surely you've discovered by now that *none* of the *normal* housing agents in this area have what you are looking for? That's because there is only *one* agent in the whole of Berkshire that specialises in this type of up-market professional apartment."

Stunned that no one had previously enlightened us to that fact, I immediately asked where we could find this agent. He replied, "Well, by coincidence, you've stumbled into the right town. If you go behind that mews over there, you'll find it on the third floor of that office building. Jackie won't have a sign outside, as she deals mostly by telephone with private overseas business clients who need executive accommodation in the area. Her ads go out in foreign markets – mostly North and South America. She closes her door at 5:30, so you need to go straight there if you want to catch her."

We ran all the way to the building, charged up the flights of stairs and arrived, panting, at a little loft office. I went immediately into my spiel, "We're looking for a two-bed executive flat: something light, open, airy, gracious, pristine; in some place green; convenient for train stations and highways; preferably newly remodelled..."

When I paused for a breath, she said, "Well, you've come to the right place. That's my speciality, and it's the only kind of place you Americans ever seem to want. Let me look at my books and see what I have available."

Be Certain that Grace *Can and Will* Manifest What it has Put Out For

She rifled through her files and then looked a second time. She turned to us with a puzzled look on her face and said, "I'm sorry. I was sure I had something, but I just don't have a thing that you could move into right away. If you could wait a few weeks..."

"No, we can't wait", I replied. "We start our seminar tour the day after tomorrow and we need to be settled before that. Once we're in work mode all our attention needs to be devoted to the events."

"Sorry... then I just can't help you."

"Would you check one more time... - please? Perhaps you overlooked something."

By then it was 5:22. She made a show of going back through her files, and at 5:25 turned back and shrugged, "Sorry, there's just *nothing* here." Gently, she started tidying her desk – in her gracious English way letting us know that it was time for us to leave. I looked at the clock on the wall: 5:26. She would close her office at 5:30. I kept stalling.

Kevin nudged me and mouthed silently, "Let's get out of here".

Something glued me to the spot. I had absolute trust, total faith that grace would fulfill its vision – that if it put out a specific prayer it would manifest it in the time needed. That certainty kept me firmly rooted, unable to move. I stalled some more... 5:27... The phone rang.

The agent looked up from her desk and seemed surprised that we were still there. She picked up the handset and had a short, discreet conversation. At 5:29 she put down the receiver and turned back to us. "You're never going to believe what just happened," she said. "A client of mine from Argentina, a polo player, just broke his leg and called to say he would not be coming to England for the polo season. He won't be able to take the flat he had booked until three months' time, so it's become available for that period. It's *everything* you want: in fact it's brand new, never before lived in. They've remodelled a Georgian stable block and fitted huge stained-glass windows in the living room – it looks stunning; it couldn't be more green, it's on the property of a golf course – and it's exactly in your price range."

We moved in the next day.

When you get very specific you allow grace to guide you to the perfect solution, and you can only follow the breadcrumbs of that guidance if you have absolute *certainty* that the infinite is capable of manifesting what it put out for.

We would never have found this unique boutique agency if we had not said *no* to every compromise that presented itself that day. In our willingness to stay true to truth, to the vision that grace had laid out, we were led perfectly, and in time, to the ideal result. In fact, the property was even better than the one we had envisioned. Only grace could have synchronistically guided us to be in that specific office at the exact moment the call came in. Truly, the infinite is magical in its ability to manifest the abundance it writes down. And it feels wondrous to participate in the magic of it all.

Following the Breadcrumbs

It is not always immediately clear which breadcrumbs we should follow, which options we should take in life, particularly when multiple possibilities are open to us. And we might feel prompted to ask, "How do I know which suggestion to follow, which lead to take, when so many options are available?"

This is when a deeper listening is being called for. As a shark in the ocean of trust, I am certain that it is not my job to create *anything*. My job is to stay alert, open to what life is presenting, knowing that any clue might lead me to the result I am seeking. I like to believe that the universe can speak to me through any person, any life situation, and I do not know who grace is going to speak through or where life is going to point me. Any moment could offer me the breadcrumbs that eventually lead me to my end result. So when multiple possibilities present themselves, I avoid consulting my mind – at all costs. I know that if I give credence to my thoughts they will only lead me into a morass of confusion.

I know that the only true, inspired answer always lies somewhere deeper than my mind, in something prior to mind, in the infinite intelligence of my own essence. But how do we get access to our essence, shut off our inner dialogue, and get still enough to be aware of divine instructions?

Trust the Body: It Never Lies

What I do is stop, take some deep breaths and turn my awareness inside. I allow myself to open and get still. I know *my body is the barometer of my own soul.* I also know that the body never lies. And though my mind can spin out of control into endless questions, justifications and options, my body is more clear, more direct, more reliable. It simply and instinctively signals me, and points me to the right course of action. So I focus my awareness on the front of my body, and I ask a simple question, for example: "Should I take option one or option two?" I keep breathing smoothly, bringing all my attention to the wordless answer that inevitably arises from within. I picture option one, and then I take a breath into the front of my chest or my solar plexus or gut. If I get a sinking feeling, or a contraction, or some sort of choking feeling, I get it that it is intuitively saying, "Not at this time", or perhaps, "Never". If however, when I ask the question I get a feeling of ease, of neutrality, of peace, then I *know* I have a green light, a go ahead, and that I can plunge into action without looking back, choosing option one as a direction to go in.

Then I ask the same question of option two. Again, I focus on the front of my body, checking if there is some kind of clutching sensation, some hesitation or glitch. If there is, I know it is a signal, "Don't go there". If, however it feels free, easy-breezy, natural, then I know that this is a door through which I can easily sail.

The soul cannot speak to you verbally. It can only communicate through the instinctive impulses of your body. If words arise in your awareness, just know that they are the product of your ego-mind, which may be pre-empting the process, overriding your natural instinct by answering the question from the surface level of the mind. But if in openness all focus goes to your body, your body intuition can be trusted to accurately signal you as to which direction to move. Your body is an unerring instrument of your soul.

And *each moment* offers the opportunity for you to check in with yourself, to be open, present and alert to the clear signals the body gives you.

I had a rather dramatic experience of how blatant the body can be when it wants to keep us on the right track.

After completing the manuscript for my first book, The Journey, five top U.K. publishers expressed keen interest in publishing it. As neither of us were familiar with the publishing industry, we asked some friends for advice. They all concurred that we needed an agent, and that the book would need to go to an auction that would involve all five publishers.

While interviewing with each of the publishing houses, I had met one editor at Harper Collins, who really impressed me. Carole was absolutely radiant, and she had come to some of The Journey seminars, and was moved by the power of the work. She said, "Brandon, I will champion this book. It's an important book. It needs to go out to humanity." Though she was my personal favourite among all the editors I had met, I knew that the auction process would be a quite impersonal one – whichever publisher bid the highest would publish the book.

A friend had given me the name of a well-known agent, one who specialised in nonfiction literature. He had recently negotiated the biggest ever U.K. advance for a book in this field, and he was known to be a savvy, hardnosed negotiator.

Kevin and I immediately got an interview with him, figuring we would start at the top. We had not taken the time to vision quest an agent, as it seemed to us that we just needed someone to perform a function as an auctioneer, and we figured that one agent was probably as good as the next.

So, with open hearts and high expectations, we went to this agent's office at a very posh London address. When we shook hands, something inside me just sank. Thinking we were novices, he launched into a treatise on the 'long road to publishing'. He told us that we needed a book proposal, and that the manuscript would have to be anglicised. The more he droned on, the more I got agitated. Finally, when I could get a word in edgeways, I said, "Stop. We don't need a book proposal. Five of the top publishers in London have already faxed through contract proposals to us. All we need you to do is to manage an auction".

As if he had not heard a word I said, he carried on ponderously listing the publishing procedures, and he said he would have to read the manuscript to see if it was worthy of publishing! Again, I reiterated that five respected publishers had all read it, loved it, and wanted to publish it. Once again he droned on about publishing protocols.

When Kevin and I walked out of his office we were sick at the thought of even contemplating working with such a stuffed up, pompous man who seemed incapable of listening. Both our bodies had been actively signalling us from the minute we shook hands and if we had taken action based on our instincts, we probably would have thanked him for seeing us and walked out straight away.

We went back home and decided to get crystal clear about the *kind* of agent that grace wanted for us – clearly it was not just somebody who could do the best deal. Once we were open in the boundless field, the intention that fell onto the page was for an agent who would champion the work because they believed in it; one who would want to get the book published for all the right reasons – even if they didn't get top dollar for it – grace wanted someone who understood the work and would get behind it.

Three days later our friend Mark called out of the blue. He seemed very excited: "You'll never guess what; I've just been to the London Book Fair and I met the most extraordinary publishing agent. He's a New Yorker who works solely with strong female authors who have an important message to get out to humanity. I thought he might be perfect for you."

I said, "You're kidding! There are actually agents out there who are that specific?" I called the number Mark gave me, and an affable New York accent came back at me, "Hi, Brandon… Ever since I saw your picture all over London, I've always known I was going to work with you. I wondered when I was going to hear from you. How can I help you?"

I shared with him the names of all the publishing houses and the editors who were interested in the book and in less than twenty-four hours it went into auction. Then a curious thing happened. Harper Collins with my favourite editor, was the under-bidder and the auction was won by a different publishing house, Hodder and Stoughton.

During the next week, I kept getting spontaneous clenching feelings in my gut. Every time I thought about signing a contract with Hodder, my heart sank. Finally I called New York and said to my agent, "I don't know what's going on with Hodder. I know they are fabulous publishers, yet every time I think about signing the contract I get a sinking feeling". There was a long pause on the other end of the phone, a big sigh, followed by, "You female authors with your women's intuition... I can always count on you throwing a spanner into the works".

"I don't know what it is... I don't know why... I just don't feel right about it. Can you fly over here and let's meet with Hodder's directors? I need to find out what is causing this."

He sighed again and said he needed to come to London anyway; that he'd be on a flight within forty-eight hours.

When we had our meeting with Hodder everything suddenly became clear. The senior editor who was head of the department assigned to my book, had recently given birth to a child who was experiencing serious health challenges. She didn't know when she would be able to work with me on the manuscript.

I turned to the senior director and said, "I'm in the mind-body healing field. This book is all about healing and awakening, and there is no way that I would want to pull a mother away from her child in order for her to focus on my book. All of her attention needs to be given to saving her child's life. I would hate to think that while she is working with me something could happen to her baby. It just isn't the right time for her to be working on a new author's book. Please, is there any way you can let us gracefully bow out of the contract?"

Graciously, he did. And that meant the book went to the next highest bidder, Harper Collins and Carole; and she turned out to be everything I would ever have wanted in an editor. She was the real champion that book needed.

Each step of the way my body was signalling me loud and clear – even if it did not make sense, even if I did not know why – and by listening to my own essence, the intended goal came effortlessly and gracefully to fruition.

We cannot always understand the mystery of the machinations of grace. What we *can* do is listen to the signs, follow the breadcrumbs and trust that the divine plan will be revealed in grace's own time. We can keep taking action, and more action, and if we stay open and tuned in to our bodies, life will let us know clearly when we are on track, and when we are not.

Open Flexibility

Over the years I have learned how important it is to be absolutely open and flexible, willing to change direction spontaneously and instantaneously.

Once the infinite has clearly laid out your precisely worded positive intention, and while you are that shark in the ocean of trust, you must remain open to the possibility that the outcome will not come in the way that you *thought* it would. Sometimes when people have vision quested they get blinkered into some sort of tunnel vision that manifestation is going to happen in a particular way, according to their precise plan. Grace's machinations are more fluid than that! If we try to tramline events into our perfectly constructed sequence of how it should all come together, we can end up overlooking the simple solution that was right there in front of our face – just because it did not appear in the *form* we *thought* it would. So it is important to stay open and flexible, and to remain *innocent* in this unknowable mystery. You can't know *how* things are going to take place, only that they *will* take place according to grace's divine unfathomable plan. All you can do is surrender and like a dog on a leash, let yourself be guided by life.

I have experienced on a few occasions that grace changed its mind. It took me on a path that opened a whole host of doors, only to decide it did not want that outcome anymore. Interestingly, years later, when I have looked back at the whole puzzle, I saw that it all made perfect sense. I had to learn the lessons I needed to learn by following one route, so I could be fully prepared for the *new* course of action that grace pointed me into.

We have to be willing to change on a dime and to constantly re-open with the vision to investigate if this current course of action is still the one the infinite wants us to take.

Kev and I have had several powerful lessons in the importance of inner listening each moment while staying open to the magic and welcoming it to appear in any form. And even when grace delivered its intended outcome, we had to remain flexible as it changed its mind about when and how. Life really called upon us to trust that an impossible seeming goal would be made manifest.

Staying Open to the Magic of Grace: The Impossible Made Possible.

Eighteen months after moving to the UK, our business had expanded and it was clear we needed to take on several staff to support the increasing demand for Journey seminars in Britain. As we were both very active in the day-to-day running of the business, we needed to move to a much larger space that included a supportive office for the staff as well as personal accommodation for ourselves. By this time our course curriculum had expanded, and the full seven-course Practitioners Programme was just getting underway. Wherever we moved would ideally have a 'great hall'; a living room large enough to double as a seminar room that could comfortably accommodate up to one hundred people. It should also have extra processing space for the participants of our advanced courses.

So once again, after clearing all our obstacles with an Abundance Process each, we sat down to vision quest. And what poured onto our pages was a gracious mansion-like house with spacious lawns – light and airy; high ceilings; lots of windows; close to London; convenient; accessible, but not in the 'dormitory-style' suburbs – some place rural or semi-rural. The living room needed to accommodate grad meetings and seminars, and a huge conservatory kitchen was required so the staff could congregate for lunch, without feeling cooped-up during the rainy and dark winter months. The separate office needed to be sunny and light, and for our one-to-ones we wanted a room that was gracious, pristine and supportive. We needed a minimum of three extra bedrooms for our live-in office manager and our guests. Kevin also needed a private study to work from. What we envisioned was a centre, a real home for The Journey. Our vision was about seven pages long and included a sprawling back garden to allow seminar participants to take breaks on the lawns, and to have al-fresco lunches at tables in the garden. The vision was extremely precise and thorough. At the end of the list I threw in one personal request; that if it was possible, I would like some sacred art in this humongous place we would be leasing.

In reading back through our writing, we both could see that grace had put out for what was essentially a 'great house', with acres of land, somehow close to London. It was a tall order, especially as our budget was relatively modest. Essentially, what was being proposed was a mansion for the price of a normal house. It seemed that the impossible was being requested by grace.

But, thankfully, Kevin and I had both learned not to question what gets written down, even if on the surface it seems utterly impossible. We know that if the infinite gives birth to a prayer then it certainly has the capability of fulfilling it.

As we were on a seminar tour we could not devote a lot of time and attention to participating in the manifestation of this tall order, but nonetheless we trusted that when the time was right somehow life would lead us to it, and we stayed open to any breadcrumbs that might show us the way forward.

It was April, and we knew that we needed to move in by August 1st at the latest, so that we could get the entire place set up and ready for our

Autumn tour, which started September 1ˢᵗ. Though we put out our prayer to friends and scoured the local classified ads and housing magazines, nothing presented itself. Either the houses were much too small or far more expensive than our budget allowed. In fact, when looking for all of the specifications of the vision, the cheapest place we could find was two and a half times what we could afford!

Grace: the Wholistic Provider

But we had learned from life that grace always provides the appropriate funds for whatever project it authentically requests. And we had learned that The Journey could and would only expand to the degree that those finances allowed. Kev and I viewed ourselves as guardians of the monies that came in, and we agreed that we would not spend one penny that had not yet been provided. We would not borrow money to grow the business or to finance the house. Yet when the universe put out that humungous vision, the budget seemed restrictively small.

Most people would have thought we were 'pie-in-the-sky' dreamers to even imagine a property of that size could come in at our modest budget. But we had learned to trust in the magic of grace to turn the impossible into the possible.

Listen to Life as if Listening to God

Then one day at work, our dear friend – now fellow director – Gaby was having a cup of tea with me on a break. Gaby asked if I might join her for a social visit to her friend, Sarah, who had recently read The Journey book. I was surprised that Gaby suggested such a thing: she knew my downtime was very precious and that I could rarely afford time to socialise. I got ready to dismiss the suggestion, when I heard my internal voice say, "Listen to life as if listening to God. You never know who you are supposed to meet or why". So I asked Gaby to give me a moment as I tuned into my body and asked if I should meet her friend. Surprisingly, I felt a deep ease at the prospect, and I realised I was being given the green light to go ahead.

When I stepped into Sarah's huge conservatory kitchen and looked out onto the glorious lawns of her typically English country garden complete with apple orchards and a fishpond, I was totally enchanted. Here we were less than half an hour from London, but it seemed light-years removed from the hustle bustle of the city, and ages away from the mind-numbing sameness of the suburbs.

She opened the double doors into her great hall with cathedral ceilings, and I gasped as I looked through a wall of french windows out to her expansive lawns. The exquisite living room was adorned with sacred art from all over the world: her husband had spent many years abroad and had become a connoisseur and collector of eclectic religious and devotional art.

We sat down to have the required cup of English tea, and I couldn't hold myself back any longer. I said, "Sarah you're not going to believe this but Kevin and I have written seven pages describing what is essentially your house. What an extraordinary coincidence!"

I shared with her that The Journey was looking for a new home, one that would be a real base for the work and I told her that I felt I was visiting her just to see that such houses did exist in England. She told me the house had been much smaller before her husband had turned their massive warehouse/garage into the sumptuous living room we were now sitting in. John had spent a lot of time in America and he liked the large open rooms there. I exclaimed, "That's why it looks so different from the front! From the driveway it seems like a nice-sized four bedroom house, but once you get to the back of it, it expands out like a fan. It's fabulous!"

After tea she took me on a house tour and showed me the sunny separate offices that John used when he was in the country. On the second floor she showed me the large suite-like bedrooms that she and the kids used. We rounded off the tour with a stroll through the orchards, stopping by the pond to admire the koi fish.

At the end of our tour I thanked her once again for inviting me and said that it was an inspiration to see my 'dream house' in actual physical form. I asked her if she knew anyone who was looking for a long-term lease on a place like hers starting August 1st, and she sighed and said she was sorry but she didn't know anyone that had anything like it.

"It's a shame because we are planning to move to America in the summer of next year. It would mean so much to me to think that someone of your calibre, someone who would treat the place like a temple, would be in our family home. I'd love to think that the house would be used consciously to serve humanity. You do such beautiful work, and it would be such a perfect place for The Journey to flourish."

I thanked her and sighed, saying, "Well I guess it must not be meant to be, I need to move by August 1st, and you're not moving out until *next* summer. We are like a pair of star-crossed lovers – our timing is off. But at least I know it's possible". I signed her copy of The Journey book and went home, quite dazed by the revelation, astounded at the uncanny resemblance this house had to the detailed vision that had found its way into our journals.

Some weeks went by and though Kevin and I looked at a few houses, nothing seemed even close anymore. Sarah's house was just so perfect! I was in love with it. Eventually, I said to Gaby, "Listen I know you're going to see Sarah on the weekend. Would you tell her I've been dreaming about her house?"

"You want me to tell her you've been dreaming about her house? That's a pretty weird thing to ask me to do."

"Well I have... Will you tell her?"

"OK. I'll pass on the message." Later that day Gaby came back to me with a quizzical expression on her face. She said, "You're not going to believe this, but I just spoke to Sarah on the phone. She asked me to tell you that ever since we had tea, she's been dreaming about *you*. She says you're welcome to call her, as she finds it uncannily coincidental".

I called, and Sarah shared that when I left her home, she kept pondering how she could make it possible for our schedules to work together. She so much wanted her house to be used for something that served life and helped people. Finally she said, "Let me talk to John – see if when we put our heads together we can come up with a plan".

She came back to me two days later: "I've spoken with John and he agrees with me that it would mean a lot to have conscious tenants who would honour our family home, so he's made a suggestion to me. At the end of the summer, when it's time for the kids to go back to boarding school, I could take a holiday home near Windsor for a couple of weeks. Then I could go stay in our vacation villa in Spain, and the kids could come join me on their half-term breaks and Christmas holidays, and John could join us from The States. That way you could move in at the end of the kids' summer holidays.

My heart started to race at the possibility, but suddenly I remembered our modest budget. "Sarah, this is such a generous offer, it takes my breath away. But I need to be honest with you; we have a very modest budget for this project and I don't want to insult you with what we could offer. If you really think you would be open to having us you would need to get a rental evaluation from an estate agent. I fear we probably couldn't touch it."

She had that done and a couple of weeks later told me the going rate for her house. My heart sank. "Oh, Sarah, that's nearly two and a half times what we could afford. We can only spend..." I named the amount.

There was a long pause at the other end of the phone as she took that in. "Whoa! We're not even in the same ballpark. I had no idea that your budget was that small."

"I'm so sorry Sarah, that's what I feared. I'm so grateful you wanted to have The Journey there, and clearly it's just not meant to be. At least it gives me hope that there is something out there, even if it can't be your magnificent home."

There was another long pause then she said, "Leave it with me. I need to talk to John".

Later that week she called again, breathless with good news. She'd spoken to John and together they had decided that they would let us have it at our price. They wanted this to be an investment they made in life, as a contribution to healing and awakening in England.

I was stunned, moved beyond words, and at first I couldn't say anything. Finally, I shared with her what a blessing that would be, and how grateful we were, and that we would treat their home as if it were a temple or monastery, keep it 'spit-polish' clean. We would cherish the blessing she was offering us.

Sarah said, "OK, so we need to speak about the move-in date. My kids have grown up here, and this will be our family's last summer holidays at this home, so I can't give it to you until September 1st, a month later than you wanted".

I paused on the other end of the line, I *never* compromised a vision that grace had written, and it had spelled out the date precisely: August 1st. This would give us the time needed to move in and set up; re-decorate this house with a fresh coat of paint, polish all the floors, clean the hundreds of windowpanes. This would not be a small task as it was a large house, and as Kev and I would be doing *all* this preparation on our own, we would likely *barely* complete the job by September 1st, when our next tour started. We needed every available moment. I hesitated before I replied and my heart sank.

"Sarah, I'm so sorry, but I'm afraid that won't work. We won't be able to take you up on your dazzling offer after all. We'll need every minute available to get the house pristine and re-decorated prior to the tour. Once it starts we won't have one moment free to devote to moving, unpacking and setting up. I absolutely understand your need to spend your last summer here in your family home. I would want to do the same if I were you. It's just that our schedules don't match, and I can't see a healthy compromise here."

Sarah paused on the other end of the line. I could only surmise she must be thinking how ungrateful I was to turn down the huge boon she was offering. But then she asked, "What if I met you half way? We'll move out August 15th and I'll take the kids to Spain for the final two weeks".

I hesitated again. How could I explain to her that when grace had put out a vision I didn't feel I had the right to compromise it; that it always had a reason and a purpose for writing what it did.

Listen to your Heart: Never Betray Grace's Intention

I was silent, trying to find a kind way to gracefully extricate myself from the situation. "Sarah... Wait a minute... Let me take a moment for something... I'll be right back".

I put the phone on the couch, and closed my eyes and tuned into my body. My body would know if flexibility was being called for, or if I needed to be steadfast in upholding grace's original crystal clear intention.

Once I got quiet I turned my awareness inside and scanned the front of my body asking, "Is it OK to move in on August 15th?" There was a pause and then my stomach clenched, giving me the unmistaken "no go" message. Ah well. It had seemed a beautiful blessing, if only for a short time. I knew better than to belie my own soul. *Every single* time I'd gone against my gut response in the past, I'd ended up in trouble. I'd be at the bottom of the mountain and I could look back up to the top and see the *exact* moment I betrayed my heart and overrode what the infinite wanted. The quickest way to failure was to go against my gut instinct. That wasn't something I could do to The Journey.

I walked back over to the couch preparing myself to turn down one of the most generous gifts life had ever graced me with, but as I picked up the phone something caused me to hesitate.

Be Open to the Changing Call of Grace

I stopped, put the phone down again and felt a pull calling me to inner listen once more; to somehow open wider. So freshly I asked the question, "Can we move in August 15th?" I re-scanned my body. As I tuned in more deeply, a picture flashed before me – one of all the trainers and beloved friends of The Journey coming together, and singing while painting the vast expanses of walls, polishing floors and cleaning windows – it was a real 'whistle-while-you-work' scene, with many hands easily accomplishing in under two weeks what would have been four weeks of drudgery for Kev and me.

The front of my body opened up and my heart felt like it was singing. The message was loud and clear: if we asked our trainers to help us prepare the new home for The Journey, we would sail through the project, and though August 15th would be cutting it fine, it was workable, doable. Grace had called me to open wider, listen deeper, and I had responded to the call and gotten a new fresh vision. "Sarah, that is so generous of you. Absolutely! We'll find a way to make it work. We would be thrilled to move in August 15th!"

What a gift! We moved in mid-August and it happened just as I had pictured: friends of The Journey came together in a real atmosphere of fun and service; we played various uplifting songs and chants from different spiritual traditions, and we painted our love and blessings into the walls, polished our good prayers into the floors, and lifted the atmosphere of the whole house making it 'sing' with our good wishes.

What a teaching of constant inner listening! First my body had signalled a definite *no* to the August 15th date, but then I had listened to that little 'tug' before I got back on the phone, a tug that was calling for a bigger opening from me. Once I had really opened, a new graceful, joyous way forward presented itself. Life was demanding I be open each moment to the changing call of grace.

When participating in the dance of manifestation, we must listen *freshly* each moment and be ready to take conscious *flexible* action as an *immediate* response to the call of the heart. *Your body is the barometer; the instrument of your own soul,* and your job is not to manifest *anything*. Your only job is to inner listen to the gut instinct that is available to you each moment, and then to *respond* through guided conscious action, flexibly *re-adjusting* whenever needed.

Healthfully Dealing with Obstacles

Our experience is that all of life is pervaded with grace. So if an obstacle is put in our way, we have to trust that *grace put it there for a reason*, that it is a divine signpost.

My past training had previously taught me that when someone said no to me, I had to find a better question to ask: I *asked until* I got a yes. And if life closed a door in my face, I had learned to *go until* I got the result I was seeking. Even if it meant knocking the door down, I needed to prove to life that nothing could get in my way, that nothing could stop me.

But I have come to realise that this ego-based approach to manifestation rarely gets wholesome results. While we give all our attention and energy to blasting down a door that simply will not open, we end up overlooking the other door to its left, one that we could have waltzed through.

So if I am presented with a steadfast obstacle, instead of banging my head against its immovable solidity, I open my whole being and look around. I know the obstacle is probably there for a reason, and I may have to learn something more before walking effortlessly through that particular door. I turn away and like water flowing around a rock in the stream, I flow into the direction that *is* open to me. A locked door doesn't mean that you will *never* walk through it, it just means *not now*.

Grace is Effortless: Struggle is Ego at Work

If you are *struggling*, trying with all your will to force something into happening, recognise it is time to *stop*, breathe and step back. Look around and be open to whichever direction grace might be calling you, and choose a more effortless route. Grace is effortless by nature. If you are on track, in flow, things fall together easily, smoothly. If you feel stymied, stuck, and start getting pushy, it's a signal that somehow you are trying to do it *your* way, the way of the ego. *Any* struggle is a sign that your *ego* is at work. This can feel like pushing a boulder up the hill: it is difficult and effortful. And the quickest way to slow down manifestation, or bring it to a grinding halt, is to let your ego take charge. When we fight the flow it is almost as if grace decides to take a back seat. It says, "Oh, so they think they are in charge? Let's see how easily this manifests then". And manifestation just gets more and more difficult until it becomes a constant uphill battle.

If there is an obstacle in your way, ask what if it was put there by life to point you in a different more healthy direction. What if all obstacles were not your enemies but your friends in manifestation, your signposts pointing you in other opportune directions?

Staying in the flow of grace means being willing and able to change direction as soon as an obstruction blocks your way.

Following a Breadcrumb that Gets a Seemingly Dubious Result

Sometimes you can follow another person's advice, check your body, and absolutely *know* that you are supposed to go through a particular door, only to find later that it didn't give you the result you *expected*. I have experienced this on numerous occasions. But six months later, when

I look back, I can see *exactly* why I *wasted* my time investigating that particular opportunity: it inevitably taught me some important life lessons that eventually prepared me for the door I am currently walking through. Every breadcrumb you follow will give you something that you need on your path to manifestation. All of it is part of the learning you need to achieve the goal that was intended. If you view everything that life puts in your path as part of your journey to abundance, each moment in life will become a more and more refined teaching that will ultimately catapult you in the direction you are meant to go.

Divine Obstacles Lead to Divine Timing

It has been our experience that when an intention arises from openness and surrender, the answer to that prayer can arise simultaneously. It can feel like the request and its resolution are one and the same in consciousness; that the *result* is already *inherent* in the asking.

At other times, particularly when our intentions have been larger or more strategic ones, it appears that consciousness shifts and begins working with divine timing to create the changes in the universe that are necessary for our exact vision to be realised. It can seem like the immediate effect of putting out our vision is to topple the first domino in a complex chain of events. Then our job is to stay open and engaged in the process, trusting that the prayer will unfold in due course, with perfect timing, and knowing that we may encounter some divine obstacles on our route.

Embracing Divine Obstacles

After some years of living in the London area of England, I began to long to spend more time with my son Mark, who was aged nine. He lived in south Wales, my original home, which was about 150 miles away from our beautiful Journey centre and home. Brandon and I had also become tired of living in the bustle of our business environment, and we wanted to breathe some cleaner, fresher sea air each day. So we decided we would buy a house for the two of us in a picturesque part of the Welsh coastline, and The Journey team would find separate accommodation in that same area.

We followed all the manifestation protocols and put out our joint intention: we wanted to live in a three-bedroom house in a specific coastline community. We described the house's features in detail. We laid out how we wanted to feel as we lived in our new home; our highest priority was an elevated position with stunning, open sea views. Then we handed the responsibility for the vision over to the universe.

We knew that we were headed for a small seaside village where the homes with the best, uninterrupted sea views seldom changed hands – and that when they did come on to the market they usually sold quickly. In order to find our perfect house we would have to be in the right place at the right time; yet we often worked abroad for weeks or even months at a time. So we told our plans to friends and family who lived in south Wales, and asked them to keep their eyes and ears open for us, and we registered with the local estate agencies.

Our top priority was a *plot* with soaring sea views and we were open to having to make adjustments, re-modelling or even knocking down an existing house, to re-build our version.

While in Australia we received an excited phone call from a friend, she had found a place with soaring sea views and put a hold on it until our return. Though the house did not fit all our specifications, we could see how we could make it work. And yet, if we were totally honest, we had wanted the house to face in a different direction so we would have a particularly picturesque view that included the rugged cliffs and jagged coastline that made this part of Wales so spectacular. We began to go through the process of buying the property and grace threw a divine obstacle in our way. We found the approach to the house was not legally owned by the property, and that at any time our neighbours could close off our right of way. So we gracefully pulled out of that project and once again opened to allow life to guide us to our goal.

Out of the blue, an estate agent who was an old acquaintance told us about a property that had not yet come onto the market. It was facing the direction we wanted and its view was more unobscured. The doctor who owned the house was building a new one in a distant village, and he was planning to move out as soon as it was ready, which he thought would be in a few months time. We had right of first refusal. It seemed like a real find as it came in at a price the we could *just* afford, and it seemed like grace had just dropped it in our laps. Patiently we waited... and waited... and then waited some more.

The Stalling Tactics of Grace

The doctor's new house took ages to finish, and Brandon and I began to wonder what was grace up to. It seemed to be stalling the fulfilment of our vision for some reason. After six months, we were still no closer to moving in, so we let the house go. We opened freshly and asked life to guide us to our dream property.

We had secretly wanted a property that had nothing in its way; with no other houses, no one else's land to obscure any aspect of our view. We wanted to be perched on a cliff-top with 180 degree views of that staggeringly beautiful seascape and still no house with views had become available during those many months that we had been looking, nor had we found any single house – available or not – that completely fulfilled that dream.

Two weeks later Brandon and I were taking a cliff-side walk and ended up on a breathtaking beach and gazed up the coastline and both of us exclaimed at once, "Oh my God! That's our property!" We would never have seen it except from this exact angle, this particular aspect, this exact spot. Hidden away, at the end of a tiny lane was a house perched on a cliff-top, completely on its own, with only uninhabited common land between it, the cliffs, and the open sea beyond. It had broad, stunning views. Having scoured all local newspapers and real estate magazines, we knew it was not on the market but we both agreed, "If there was one property in the whole of Wales, in fact in the whole of Britain, that we would want to live in, it's that one. Shame its not available. If it ever came on the market we would buy it in a heartbeat".

The *next morning* we got the latest property newspaper, and lo and behold that little house was freshly listed. We immediately called the estate agent, who was on his way to put up the *For Sale* sign, and within three hours we had negotiated a price and bought our *perfect* house.

Grace: the Divine Manipulator

What was extraordinary about it all is that grace had to stall us over the first house, which then led us to the second home, and while we were patiently waiting, our budget expanded to a level where we could finally afford the third house. And grace manoeuvred us into taking a walk to see this hidden gem, the *night* before it went on the market, so that we could be the first customers to snap it up.

Our chances of being in the country, in that place, at that particular time, were next-to-nil, and yet life had conspired with huge machinations for our dream house to fall into our lap. And instead of fighting the way of grace we just went with the flow, allowing ourselves to be innocently, spontaneously guided to the perfect result.

Be Content to Live in the Mystery

Sometimes life will put you through a puzzling path whose mystery you won't understand until all the puzzle pieces come together and then voilà, the whole picture, the divine timing, the obstacles, the stalling tactics all make sense in the end.

The learning was loud and clear: stay open and let yourself be guided even when you do not understand the mysterious workings of grace.

Celebrate Your Achievements: Keep Score of the Gifts that Manifest

It is very important that once you manifest something you take time to celebrate its arrival, and that you keep score. So often, once a particular result is attained or an achievement is realised, we barely notice its presence, and we do not stop to rejoice in its blessing before we move onto the next goal. Remember that grace is drawn to a grateful heart, and more is added to the one who appreciates and is grateful for the gift they have been blessed with. If, instead of recognising the bounty of life, you treat its generous gifts casually, life can start to get disinterested in blessing you. It is as if it says, "Oh, I guess they don't really *care* about that relationship; they didn't really *want* that job; they don't really *value* that car, that home; they don't *appreciate* their healthy body. They were given what was asked for and it doesn't really matter to them. Maybe it should go to someone who is more grateful; to someone who will really honour the gift". And the very things you worked so hard to achieve can start falling away from you.

Nearly every day during our conversations, Kevin and I are naturally led to how blessed we are, how lucky we are, how thankful we are. It is not that we make a practice of it; it is just that we are aware that any material things in life are truly a gift from grace, and we feel naturally grateful for our good fortune. *It has become our nature to celebrate life, to keep score of the blessings in life*. And our gratitude seems to draw even more blessings to it.

So once you have successfully achieved a result, take the ongoing time to celebrate it, honour it, to thank life for it. It is important to recognise how lucky you are and to express gratitude for being blessed with the play-dough of life.

Honouring and Cherishing Life's Gifts

We feel that part of our way of thanking life for its bounty is by honouring and caring for whatever it is that has manifested. Our gratitude is expressed through our *actions*. If we have been blessed with a new car, we feel that the way to honour it is to have it serviced, cleaned, waxed and cared for. If we have been blessed with family or friendships, we invest time in developing them, helping them blossom. If a house has been given to us by life, we honour it, keeping it in immaculate condition, repairing it immediately when repairs are needed. Even our clothes are treated with great respect, and are cleaned and freshly ironed each time before they are worn. Every action you take to care for, honour or cherish your relationships, your material things, your job, signals that you are *still* grateful, still blessed by the gift given to you. Life *gets it* that you truly cherish what you have been given, and it naturally wants to add more to those who honour life.

But if *you* treat your bounty with little or no *interest*, letting relationships grow fallow, your house get seedy, your job get stale, very soon life will get the clear message that you don't really *value* the gifts that have been given to you, and it can start taking things away. So to participate in healthy abundance make sure you celebrate and keep score of your great good fortune and honour it by cherishing and caring for it.

The Power of Non-Attachment

There is still one more principle of manifesting abundance that needs to be addressed here: the power of non-attachment. You might say, "But how can I be non-attached? If I'm a shark in the water of life, constantly alert, on the look out, taking conscious action, how can I remain unattached? How is that possible? The two seem antithetical".

For me non-attachment is perhaps the most important part of all the principles of manifestation. I know that when an intention goes out it is not even 'my' vision; it belongs to the infinite. I am just a willing servant, letting myself be used as a vehicle participating in the dance of manifestation. The intention did *not* go out from personal need or personal greed. It went out as a non-personal vision created by my essence.

But we are all human, and as we flow into motion, sometimes craving can seep in, letting it become personal. We get so involved in the dance that we make the mistake of believing *we* are the manifestors, that all achievements are down to us, and we start to feel driven, obsessed to attain our goals. The ego co-opts all the results along the way, believing *it* has attained them all on its own, and it becomes voracious in its efforts to achieve even more.

If you find this kind of unhealthy attachment to outcomes slipping into your daily life just take a moment to stop, and breathe. Recognise that personal attachment is driving you and that it is a recipe for disappointment and disaster. Then take some time to get still and open and let the following teaching arise in your awareness.

This lesson on the power of non-attachment has been one of the most life transforming teachings I've ever experienced, in all the years on my spiritual path. It forever transformed my relationships to the material 'things and people' in my life and it is one that continues to work on me to this day.

Non-attachment: A Vital Key

About eighteen years ago, I was sitting in a meditation retreat with Gurumayi, an enlightened master who often teaches in the traditional manner through powerful stories. This particular story impacted me deeply. It crept under my skin and began to infuse my being as a *living* experience. In the hearing of it, the strings of attachment mysteriously and effortlessly began to loosen their grip and over time melted away naturally. I did not know it had happened until I was confronted by the real-life experience two years later of losing everyone and everything I loved, and finding that I still felt abundant and whole. Here is the story.

Once upon a time, a long, long time ago in India, there was an enlightened master who was also a very wealthy man from a distinguished family and the owner of several factories. He and his devoted disciple were casually strolling through a remote and dusty village one day when they came upon a shop displaying antiques, bric-a-brac, and odds and ends. There, in the shop window, was a totally unexpected item that caused the enlightened master to pause for a closer look. It was a porcelain teacup, sitting all on its own, and when he peered more closely at it, he realised it was the very same, rare, prized teacup he had been looking for for over thirty years. He already owned the first eleven teacups of this priceless tea set, the rarest of its kind, passed down from the rajas of old, and this last cup would make the set complete.

He was thrilled at his great good fortune and felt that grace had smiled upon him on this propitious day, for thirty years is a long time to be searching for a teacup.

Now the shopkeeper, standing in the shadows just out of sight, spied the enlightened master gazing at his window and his heart leapt up into his throat: "My god! He's finally turned up! This is my lucky day. Everyone knows this master is a very wealthy man. Now my wife and I can finally retire. This is the one teacup he needs to complete the rarest set in the world. We've got it made!"

As he gleefully exulted, the shopkeeper told his wife to hide in the kitchen. The gods had smiled upon them, and they could finally close the shop and take their longed-for pilgrimage to the holy city of Varanasi. They could live like kings and would never want for anything again.

As the master approached, the shopkeeper eagerly opened the door, and with a low sweeping bow, he welcomed him and his disciple into the shop. He donned his most ingratiating smile, and with a smarmy, oily voice said, "Namasté, swamiji. How can I help you today?"

The master gently explained that he was interested in the teacup in the window. "Ah, well," replied the shopkeeper, "that is my most precious piece. Perhaps you are aware that it's the rarest of its kind in the world. It belongs to a set of twelve, and it's the last one".

"Yes," said the master, "I'm very familiar with the set. It's a favourite of mine. I'd like to purchase that cup. What is your asking price?"

The shopkeeper's mouth became dry and his heart began to pound. He thought, "This swami knows the unique rarity of the cup. He'll pay whatever I say". In the excitement of the moment, the shopkeeper named an astronomical price.

Upon hearing the amount, the master simply replied, "No, kind sir, I will only pay this amount". He named a generous and equitable sum and said, "It is a fair price".

The shopkeeper was taken aback. He had thought the sale would be easier; after all, an enlightened master is not some fishmonger who haggles in the market. Disconcerted, but not too discouraged, the shopkeeper dropped his asking price by half, explaining to the master what a loss it would be to him and reiterating that it was the only remaining one of its kind.

The master acknowledged that it was true. The cup was irreplaceable – the rarest available. Then he repeated the original price he had offered and said, "It is a fair price".

Completely befuddled, the shopkeeper thought to himself in alarm, "Okay, okay. So this master wants to bargain. I'll take it down by half again, but that's it. I'll still end up a wealthy man".

With an unconvincing smile, and no excuse at the ready, he said, "Swamiji, you really do drive a hard bargain. Okay, let me tell you what I'll do. I'll reduce it by half again, but that's it – it's my final offer".

The master's face saddened a little, and in a quiet voice he replied, "I'm sorry, sir. I guess you didn't understand me. I will pay only this price. It's a fair price".

He motioned to his devotee that the time had come to conclude their stay, thanked the shopkeeper, and quietly walked out the door.

When they were but fifty paces down the road, they heard someone calling, shouting, and when they turned to look, it was the shopkeeper. He was running after them, flailing, out of breath, pleading, "Swamiji, swamiji, come back, please come back... You can have the cup at your price".

And so they returned and the transaction was completed quite amicably. Of course, the shopkeeper knew that even at the master's price, he and his wife were now set for life. The master knew this, too, and both were well pleased.

While the deal was being concluded and the teacup was being wrapped, the master's devotee noticed a magnificent sabre hanging on the wall, just above the shopkeeper's head. He could not take his eyes off it – it was the most intricately designed, yet powerful sword he had ever seen. Whenever he turned from it, he found his gaze constantly drawn back. He felt mesmerised by the sword.

He thought, "I must have it. I'll call it my 'sword of truth'. It will take the highest place of honour in my house, just above the altar. Never before have I seen such a handsome sword. I simply must have it".

"I am a man of modest means," he figured, "but if I do exactly what the master did, maybe I can get it at a vastly reduced price".

So, trying to sound very unassuming and a little disinterested, the disciple casually motioned to the sword up on the wall and said to the shopkeeper, "That's an attractive sabre you've got up there. I haven't got much use for it, but I'd like to know the asking price".

The shopkeeper looked the devotee in the eye. He was a shrewd man, and though he lived a humble life, he did not like to be toyed with. Pretence left a bad taste in his mouth. Nonetheless, he was feeling pleasantly disposed, having just made the sale of a lifetime, and he decided to be generous, naming an only slightly inflated price.

The devotee feigned a gasp, and said, "No, kind sir, I will pay only this price. It's a fair price". He imitated the master to a tee.

The shopkeeper, always happy to barter, for that was how the game was played, dropped the price.

The devotee winced, and said, "No, sir. I will pay only this price. It's a fair price". And the shopkeeper dropped the price again.

The devotee finally shrugged his shoulders and said, "I guess you didn't understand, sir. I will only buy the sword at this price. It's a fair price". And, as the master had now concluded his business, together the two quietly strolled out of the shop.

When they were fifty paces down the road, the devotee looked back to see if the shopkeeper had followed them, but the shop door remained closed. In silence he and the master continued walking. Every so often, the devotee snuck glances over his shoulder, completely nonplussed that the shopkeeper had not come chasing after him. He'd done everything the master had done. Why hadn't it worked?

A mile down the road, they paused for a drink, and the disciple finally spoke up. "Master, why hasn't the shopkeeper come running after me the way he came after you?" The master, a man of few words, remained silent.

"But why didn't he follow us?" the devotee insisted.

Finally, the master spoke. "Do you still thirst for that sword?"

"Well, yes, master," the devotee replied. "Of course I do."

"That shopkeeper can smell your thirst. He knows you lust for that sabre, and he also knows that when he opens his shop tomorrow morning, you'll be his first customer, and you'll take it at his price."

The disciple was silent for a moment, as he let the words sink in, then petulantly asked, "But master, did you not thirst for that teacup? You searched for it for over thirty years. Didn't you crave to complete your set?"

The master was silent, and in the quiet, the student realised that of course the master had not lusted for a mere cup. A little ashamed that he had been so audacious to presume that a master would crave for anything, he humbly asked, "But what is your secret, master?"

The master quietly answered, "He came after me because he knew that I genuinely meant it when I said I would take it only at a fair price – I was unattached. With you he could smell your lust, and he knows you'll be back".

"But how can you not crave a cup that completes your rarest of collections?"

"Let me tell you my secret," replied the master. "Every night before I go to bed I get down on my hands and knees, and I thank God with all my heart for all the blessings of the day. And then, with my whole being, I offer up to God everything I hold dear. I offer up my factories, my ashram, my homes. I offer up my students, my friends, and even my beloved wife and precious children — in my mind's eye I see the factories and ashram burnt down. I see my family and loved ones taken from me, and resting in God's arms. And when my prayer is finished, I go to sleep a poor man.

"When I wake up, I look around me to greet the fresh, new day, and I see God's grace is still surrounding me. And, flooded with gratitude, I get down on my knees, and I thank God with all my heart that for one more day he has blessed me with these priceless gifts. I realise that I am only His caretaker. These gifts were never mine to begin with. They have only ever been on loan. Everything is on loan."

Everything is on Loan

When I heard these words, they had a profound effect on me. They penetrated deeply, and when I arrived home after the meditation retreat, I made a silent vow to myself that I would take this teaching into my life. Like the master in the story, each night I took a few moments to truly thank life for all the blessings of the day, and offered up to grace all that was dear to me – my home, my family, my lifestyle, my marriage, my possessions, and all my material wealth. And I found that each morning I arose with a heart full of gratitude, overwhelmed that I had been blessed for yet one more day.

Have a Light Relationship with Material Things

My relationship with the physical things in my life began to take on a quality of lightness. I was fully aware that these things really didn't belong to me. They were a gift from grace, and my responsibility, or dharma, lay in cherishing them, honouring them, and savouring the blessedness of having them around me.

I also came to view my relationships differently. They took on a fuller, more spacious quality, no ownership anywhere and somehow even deepened in the letting go.

Cherishing the Gifts Life Blesses You With

Everything around me began to feel special. Everything seemed imbued with a light spaciousness. I became aware of the ephemeral nature of all things – how short a time we have on this planet, and how lucky we are to have the bountiful blessings we are surrounded with. This simple, innocent practice reverberated with ever-deeper teachings about the fleeting nature of existence and how it is our gift to cherish it while it lasts.

No Ownership

I found that an important part of the gift of cherishing what we have been given so graciously is to pass on these blessings to others. Increasingly, I noticed that while the material things in my life came and went gracefully, the completeness and gratitude in which I rested remained untouched. After a while, it became clear there was no ownership abiding anywhere – just life dancing in a vaster context of grace.

A paradox unfolded in my life. There was the profound recognition that everything was a blessing to be cherished, and yet, with the recognition that it was all on loan, there was also a totally non-personal acceptance of letting the cherished things pass out of my life and into others' hands if grace so desired. I loved each gift dearly, yet felt completely neutral and unattached in its leave-taking. As a result, I developed both a richer and a lighter relationship with the outer things in my life.

Three years after the retreat, this new awareness was tested by grace. As I mentioned earlier in this book, our family's home burned down in a huge wild fire. This house held everything that was materially dear to me – photographs; writing; mementos of family holidays; anniversary presents; inherited porcelain; beloved books; journals; and wedding pictures. Eighteen years of accumulated memories were gone, and we were financially devastated, materially wiped out.

I remember so clearly hearing the news and waiting to feel a big thud in my guts... because, of course, the truth was that we would never be able to replace any of these priceless things. I kept waiting and expecting to feel fear or anxiety over losing everything, but it didn't arise.

Instead, I felt curiously free, as if some old karma had been lifted off my shoulders – as if a huge weight had fallen away. It was true: all of those things had only ever been on loan, and the gratitude and completion I experienced was completely untouched, completely whole and abundant.

Over the years since that time, grace has blessed me with a lifestyle so charmed and full of grace that even in my dreams I could not have imagined it. And yet, I'm still aware that everything in my life *is* and *always was* on loan. I have an even lighter relationship with the outer things in my life. The gratitude deepens, along with an even sharper recognition that life is truly fleeting and each precious drop of it must be savoured. The extraordinary blessedness of life has become ever more poignant. Truly, non-attachment is your invitation to soar in the freedom of wholesome abundance.

The All-Inclusive Nature of Wholesome Abundance

Non-attachment opened my life to one of never-ending abundance. And with that openness came a natural desire to include others in that abundance, to share the grace that life had blessed me with, even if it was 'only ever on loan'. The gratitude for the magnificence of creation and the effulgence of generosity in which life embraced me, caused me to look wider than my own personal needs, wants and desires. In the wakeful presence of infinite abundance there is a wordless pull, a call to include as many people as I could within my sphere of influence. It wanted to embrace my family, friends, work relationships, even humanity. Somehow being open in a field where everything is possible and already whole, already abundant, automatically caused me to open my heart to *all of life*, all of existence.

After all, everything, all of life, is appearing in this field that is my own essence and it is only natural that I would feel guided to take care of all parts of my own self.

Openness to the Larger All-inclusive Picture

My actions naturally began to reflect this wider context of being, and caretaking all of life became as natural and intrinsic as breathing. Before taking any action, the greater whole is always taken into consideration, and seeing how the intention could benefit life is the criterion on which all my decisions and actions are based. From building an eco-home, to providing eco-cars for our employees, to carbon-offset programmes for all our team's flights, to recycling everything at work and home. From choosing seminar venues that are more *green* and carbon-aware, to caring for the personal development of each and every employee, investing in their growth, to flourishing our students, honoring our trainers, partnering our practitioners and caring for our extended family. From making sure our offices are environmentally friendly, light and supportive to our staff, to caring for our personal family members and flourishing them in abundance, to constantly developing liberating and healing work available to people from all over the globe. From translating the work into dozens of languages to co-creating Journey Outreach, and helping people to find the wholeness and peace... on and on. All decisions are based on a wholistic paradigm, where every aspect of life benefits from it.

And none of it has come from some learned formula or religious dogma, but rather it is a natural, automatic expression of wholesome abundance-consciousness. It feels inevitable, unavoidable when you are fully awake in the unobscured enlightened presence of your own soul.

In this larger context, the co-creative dance of manifestation takes on a magical quality, one where each action is a privilege, each material result a gift. In fact, each moment feels wondrous, full of grace, no matter what form it appears in. And all of it is part of you, happening *in* you.

When you are wide open in your own essence, conscious actions are simply the natural consequence. They don't occur because someone has given you a prescription for how to live life in conscious integrity, nor are they based on someone's righteous rules. It is something much simpler, more basic, more intrinsic. Caring for all of life as part of yourself, feels organic, unavoidable, as natural as laughter, as right as love. It is simply your own essence's natural expansion.

You Are Love

Love by nature is generous, all-inclusive, all accepting and to wake-up to your own essence is to realise that the love that you are permeates all of life. It *is life,* and you are that.

It is love that propels conscious action, and it flows you into healthy abundance. In fact love *is* abundance. And being part of the dance of manifestation becomes a never-ending blessing to all those around you, to life itself. Your actions are the natural expression of love, and your work is love made visible.

The Call

This love is calling *all* of us. It is asking us to *decide* that it is time to wake up, to play our part, to be part of the all-inclusive, co-creative dance of creation. Love wants to *use* you; it wants to use all that you are in your essence to contribute to life, to embrace life, to be part of the shift in consciousness our planet so sorely needs.

We are at a time in history when we can no longer deny this call. We cannot pretend we do not feel it. We are at a time when we are being asked to *use* the tools that life is providing us, to liberate ourselves and to open up to conscious abundance on all levels of being.

Love is calling you now. Love wrote this book to give you the tools to shed the shackles of your silent saboteurs, to penetrate the lies of your beliefs, and to liberate you from fear. This love is calling you into the unobscured infinite field of wakeful presence, and it is longing to propel you into conscious healthy action. It wants you to embrace all of life as your own self and it is giving you the means – these Principles of Manifestation – to participate in this glorious play of creation.

"If you let love rule your heart, there is no obstacle, no barrier, no problem you can't overcome. This is God's promise to every human being, and it is the key to liberation for us all.
Love is the most powerful force in the universe, and it is also the most available force, because everyone can tap into it." ~ Martin Luther King, Jr.

This book is an invitation from grace to be part of the wave of awakening our world needs. You are being asked to play a larger role, a bigger game, a more wholistic part in manifestation, and life is insisting that you allow all that you are to be fully expressed, fully used by grace. Creative solutions, conscious answers, inspired ideas and effulgent abundance all arise from the unobscured awareness that is your own self, and this same boundless self is inviting you to take your lampshade off. Life is calling you to stop playing small; it is beckoning you into greatness.

This is a big call. This is an important time in history. And this is your invitation to open to the enlightened consciousness our earth needs. The choices we make today will not only affect our own lives, they will not only affect the lives of our children and grandchildren; they will forever change the nature of the planet on which humanity lives.

Consciousness *is* the new currency. In fact consciousness is the *only* currency that will heal our world. It is time to wake up and begin living in conscious abundance.

Your destiny awaits you.

CHAPTER 5

The Process Work

This Chapter includes the two very powerful processes that we explored in Chapters 1 and 3. As the processes are so potent, it is best that you read the entire book before undergoing them.

The Worst/Best Fear Process – Overview

For the first process – the Worst/Best Fear Process – we strongly encourage you to set aside some private uninterrupted time where you can undergo this guided introspection in a peaceful, supportive setting. We recommend re-reading Chapter 1 to deeply familiarise yourself with the process. Chapter 1 will give you the context, framework and teaching to understand its purpose and will remind you how powerful it can be.

To begin, we recommend sitting quietly for some moments, taking a few slow, deep breaths and letting your being settle. Have the intent that you will be open and deeply honest with yourself.

In this process you will be welcoming up your worst fears about a certain area of your life. When fear arises you will innocently ask yourself, "What's the worst that could happen?" Allow your worst fears and any pictures of them to come flooding and ask, "How does that make me feel?" Then write it down on the page designed for this purpose (the Worst Fears Worksheet). Next you will ask, "If that happened, then what would happen? What's the worst that would take place?" Again a picture might arise in your awareness, and you can ask yourself, "How does that make me feel?" Then allow all the feeling to come flooding. You will keep asking and opening – feeling your way down through the various emotional layers.

Eventually, you might experience a vast nothingness, an emptiness, possibly even a death-like void. If this happens, know that this is fine – it is just another emotional layer to go through on your way into your own essence. It is natural and is part of the process. Keep going deeper into the very core of your being by asking, "What's in the heart of this?" feeling yourself opening and expanding all the while. Eventually you will arrive in a vast open expanse of pure awareness, boundless presence – this that we call 'source'.

Then, by asking the question, "Who am I?" you will be carried deeper and deeper into the expansive presence of your own essence.

Once you are resting in an ocean of awareness, you will turn to the second page and begin writing down your answers to the question, "What is the best that could happen?" Keep opening, letting the best that could happen arise in your awareness, getting more and more expansive as you ask, "If that happened, then what is the best that could happen?" Let this list become longer, stronger and more and more inspiring. Let the vision grow into one that excites you, inspires you, one that will give you the leverage you need to face down your worst (circled) fear and clear it with an Abundance Process.

Then, at a later time with a partner, you can go through the full, comprehensive Abundance Process, and you will allow your worst fear to be part of it.

This Worst/Best Fear Process alone will give you a clarity and decisiveness to want to go about the process of manifesting your highest vision for yourself. It is deeply liberating and exceedingly inspiring. By facing your worst fears, you open yourself to the possibility of allowing the best to come flooding into your life.

Instructions for Worst/Best Fear Process

During these uncertain and challenging times...

- ## What are your worst fears?

[Just relax, open your body and let all your fears arise of their own accord, giving permission for *any* emotion to come up.
Write down a list of each of your worst fears and how that makes you feel]

[Then ask yourself:]

- ## What's the worst that could happen?...

[Imagine the worst that could happen and experience how that makes you feel. Write down on your worst fear worksheet]

- ## And how does that really make me feel?...

[Just allow the feeling to come flooding... Really welcome it... As you let the feelings grow stronger, keep asking yourself the questions from the box beneath. Continue asking until your experience spacious openness, vast nothingness, pure awareness, or similar]

> - **If that happened, then what's the worst that could happen? ...** [Write down]
>
> - **And how does that really make me feel? ...** [Write down]

[Repeat questions in boxed section above until you feel completely emptied out. Then continue opening into pure awareness, vast consciousness, by asking:]

- **What's in the heart of it? ...** [Write down]
- **What's the essence of this? ...** [Write down]
- **What's revealing itself? ...** [Write down]

[Then ask repeatedly until you are resting deeply in an ocean of presence:]

- **Who am I? ... Who am I? ... Who am I? ...**
  [Write down]

[Then, when you are resting in spacious consciousness begin asking:]

- **What's the best that could happen?**
- **And if that happened, what's the best that could happen?**

[Keep opening and writing this vision down on the Best worksheet until this list is longer and stronger. Let it be inspiring!]

Worst Fear Worksheet

During these uncertain and challenging times... what are your worst fears?

What's the worst that could happen?	How does that make you feel?
(If that happened then what's the worst that would happen?)	

Who am I? List qualities.

Best Worksheet

.What's the best that could happen?

What's the best that could happen? ... If that happened, then what would happen? (Make the list longer/stronger than the worst list.)

The Abundance Process Overview

The Abundance Process is a deep, comprehensive and thorough process to help you clear various disempowering beliefs, and get to the roots, the cell memories which have limited various aspects of abundance in your life. It is a full sweep clean of various hidden comfort zones, silent saboteurs, negative beliefs and unhealthy ways of being. It takes place in four stages. To prepare for the process, you will need to have read the entire book and we recommend you re-read Chapter Three to deeply familiarise yourself with the context, content and purpose of the process.

It is a process that can only be done with a partner and, including the time for answering the elicitation questions, it can take anything from three to four hours, sometimes even more! So it requires of you a commitment to yourself to set aside the time in an appropriate, private setting so the process can unfold fully in its own natural way.

This is a process that will demand deep honesty, openness and humility, and you will have to be willing to open emotionally to how the various beliefs and cell memories make you feel. It is not a process that can be done casually, by half measures. For it to be truly effective you will have to make the decision that you will be real, authentic and emotionally available.

To begin, make sure your partner has read the book and that you both have re-read Chapter Three, and have looked through the entire Abundance Process at least a couple of times to familiarise yourself with the various stages of the script.

In Stage 1, you will undergo an elicitation where your partner will encourage you to imagine yourself in various scenarios that really push you, stretching you beyond the bounds of your comfort zones. Once you have fully imagined yourself in these 'button pushing' scenes, once you really feel as if you are actually *experiencing* them, living them fully, your partner will then start asking you a series of questions (Stage 2) that will elicit hidden disempowering beliefs and silent saboteurs related to these scenes. The questions will drive to the surface buried emotional shutdowns and limitations and negative beliefs. As you write down the answers to the questions you will likely be surprised at how much unhealthy conditioning has been stored inside.

It is important to be fully honest in your answers. Be willing to dig deep and let the limiting patterns and beliefs arise in your awareness. The process is often uncomfortable as none of us want to face the lies we have all bought into. And the invitation is for you to be open and authentic. Once you have uncovered various disempowering beliefs, limitations and patterns and written them down you are ready for Stage 3, the main process.

Pick the strongest emotion that arose for you and use that as your starting place, your emotional capstone. Once again, start opening down through the emotional layers (like you did in the Worst/Best Fear Process) fully feeling the emotions at each level. As you are opening into the core of each feeling, it is essential to **stay out of the story** – out of your analytical thoughts – and put all your attention and awareness onto **feeling the pure open emotion *in your body.***

Just feel the feeling fully, name it, and open into the next feeling. Feel that fully and allow yourself to drop through to the next feeling. You keep opening into the core from one emotional feeling to the next, until you finally experience source.

This is *not* a process about listening to your mind-talk and analysing why you are feeling what you are feeling. It simply is a purely kinesthetic process of dropping through the emotional layers, like peeling back the layers of an onion, to get to the core of your being, to source.

At the top of the sheets, the instructions advise you, whenever you see '...' to pause, and allow your partner 'sufficient' time to experience the answer to your question. Sufficient time can be anywhere from ten to fifteen seconds, sometimes even thirty seconds.

It is important to understand that the point of the process is to feel the emotions openly and, after tasting each one fully, to open into the next layer. It is not necessary, nor is it a good idea, to wallow in the emotion at every level. Nor is it advisable to describe it in detail and tell a story about it.

To access feelings, rather than consult your thoughts, just internally scan your body and find where the emotion feels strongest. It may start as a subtle sensation. As you focus your attention on it, just allow it to intensify itself. Be willing to experience the fullness of it. Keep your attention on the feeling inside your body.

Then, very simply, feel it and open into the core of it. At some point you may pass through nothingness, emptiness, even a death-like layer. This is perfectly normal. I call this layer 'the unknown zone'.

Sometimes people fear the unknown, so just remember to relax, surrender and open into whatever is next.

After you have dropped through the unknown zone, you usually will start feeling lighter and easier, and a great sense of relief will gradually spread through you.

It's important to continue opening down through the remaining levels until you reach source. You'll know when you are in source when you experience yourself as *very vast* – as a presence that is both inside and outside the body – *everywhere*.

This is a very important point to understand, because often, after dropping through the unknown zone, you will start using source-like words such as love, peace, laughter, joy, light, contentment, freedom, *but* it may still feel as if it's located somewhere *inside* the body.

When the feeling becomes very expansive, spacious – as if you are one with everything, or are a part of everything – this is a true realisation of source. When it is vast, it moves from being a simple emotion to being pure awareness itself. So continue opening into the core of each emotion until you are resting in your own essence, in a vast spacious field of pure awareness, oneness, love. Keep opening *deeper* into source by going into the heart of each emotion and *expanding* until you are in a field of all possibilities, with all of life taking place within you, with you as part of all of life. Just rest here in this field of all love, pure potential.

Then following the script, your partner will instruct you to let source 'wash up' through the layers, letting your essence speak to and 'wash through' each layer until you get to the campfire layer where the asterisk * appeared (the level where a person, picture or memory appeared while you were going down through the layers. If no picture or memory appears, your partner can pick the strongest layer and that becomes the level of the campfire). Wash through that layer and go straight to the campfire.

The campfire is a place of unconditional love where the younger you sits, dialogues, and empties out with others who have contributed to your putting a lid over your abundance potential. So at the fire will be a younger you, a present you, a mentor in whose divine wisdom you trust, and various people who have participated in causing you to put a lampshade over your light – people who contributed to you playing small, feeling diminished or shut down. There may be quite a number of people or just a few. Sometimes there will be just one person. There is no wrong or right number of people.

The purpose of this verbalised campfire is to give the younger you the opportunity to empty out all the stored pain, hurt, shame, blame, anger, self-recrimination – to release all the buried emotions and stored consciousness and unspoken words. It gives you a chance to get it all off your chest and out of your cells. This dialogue must be spoken out loud from the voice of the consciousness of the younger you, directly from the real core of the pain from that time. Then the other person at the campfire will be given permission to respond and empty out (once again do this out loud). Let the dialogue continue until all previously unspoken words and pain have been fully expressed and released. When both parties are completely empty, do the same with the present day you, letting yourself empty out and letting the other person respond until all is empty and complete.

After you are completely empty, your partner will guide you through the Change Memory Process. This is fully scripted, so just follow along. You will elicit several memories in which you were disempowered in some way, or had shut down to your own abundance potential, and you will imagine putting them onto a video screen and letting them play out the way they did play out. Then you will be given emotional resource balloons that would have helped you cope with that old scene in a healthier, more abundant way.

You breathe in the consciousness of the balloons, then you will step back onto the video screen, and this time you will play the scene the way it *would* have happened with access to all these emotional resources. This conditions your brain to respond healthily in the future. You will do the full Change Memory Process with each individual memory.

Once done, you will come back to the campfire and empty out any remaining disempowering beliefs. Then the mentor will sweep you clean of all the old beliefs and install new healthier beliefs that your partner will help you to elicit. These new truths are an antidote to the unhealthy lies you used to believe.

Then, once you are complete, you will finally forgive all people at the campfire letting the younger you forgive the others, the present you forgive the others, and letting the others forgive you for anything that might need forgiving. Finally you forgive yourself. Then the campfire will disappear and you will continue washing through any remaining emotional layers before going on to the Future Integration.

Just follow the Future Integration page. It is fully scripted and self explanatory. It is not necessary to write anything down – it is enough to just listen to it. It is your way of checking with your body and being that over time the healing will continue to evolve naturally. By six months to a year's time you should be feeling lighter, freer, easier and joyous about creating healthy abundance in all areas of your life.

Keep going until you are ten years down the line. At this point your partner will ask you to stay wide open in the consciousness of the future you, and while you are resting in that abundance-consciousness, your partner will invite you to play the scenarios that you were originally hooked by, but this time to experience them from this *new* abundance-consciousness of the future you. They will go through one or two scenarios with you and then, once your eyes are open, they will invite you to complete all the scenarios and questions, this time from the healthy abundance-consciousness of the future you.

You will now move onto Stage 4. You will play each scene and answer all questions newly.

So, the entire process comprises:

Stage 1 – Experiencing scenes that challenge your comfort zones, push your buttons, cause you to stretch beyond what is your current operational envelope.

Stage 2 – Asking the questions to elicit unhealthy, negative beliefs and memories related to these scenes.

Stage 3 – Undergoing the full Abundance Process:
    a)   Going down through the layers to Source
    b)   Washing back up the layers
    c)   Going to the campfire
        •   Everyone empties out
        •   Change Memory Process
        •   Change Beliefs Process

- Sweep Clean Process
- Forgiveness
- Campfire disappears

a) Washing up through remaining layers
b) Future Integration Process, including a couple of scenarios with questions.

Stage 4 – Opening eyes and experiencing all the old scenarios from the new abundance consciousness, playing each scene individually and answering the questions before going onto the next scene.

Voilà! – You are finished!

Congratulations! As you can see this is a *very* comprehensive clean-out and fully worth it. You should feel inspired, ready and able to manifest healthy, conscious, ethical abundance in your life!

Stage 1:

Elicitation Scenarios – Some Examples You Can Use.

Here are examples of some scenarios that will elicit unaddressed emotions and beliefs. Get your partner to read them out to you. Some questions will evoke strong emotional responses, others less so, and that is fine. Be willing to go with and explore fully those questions that produce the strongest results, and you can ignore those that don't work for you [and be sure you are being real, telling the deepest truth in this]. It is fine to alter or adapt any of the scenarios to make them more personal to you or potent for you – just bear in mind that the goal is to evoke a genuinely strong emotional response.

Add to the scenarios yourself by opening and genuinely enquiring what sort of [real or imagined] personal or work situations or stretches would begin to push your emotional buttons. There are loads of circumstances in life that emotionally trigger us, so just be willing truthfully to explore. [Remember to stay blame-free. Your emotional response is your own responsibility, so just allow yourself to feel the pure emotions and stay out of any associated story.]

Where the question asks for a step-by-step increase in time or money, make sure to take sufficient time to open and explore this in increments, so you can identify the point at which you first begin to feel uncomfortable or agitated.

For each scenario open emotionally and identify the feeling that comes up for you. Your partner will read out one scenario at a time [from this sheet, or your own scenario] and ask the questions from the Elicitation Questions & Answers Sheet [next page]. You will write down the answers starting with box 1A and working across the sheet and writing your answers in the appropriate boxes. For the second scenario, move down to box 2A, and so on. [You may photocopy this sheet, or just make a rough copy of it so you can write your answers down.]

Manifesting Abundance

1.   A friend, acquaintance or organisation [you decide which] is willing to make a large low-interest or interest-free investment in your organisation, business or personal career [you decide which]. They are willing to be flexible in negotiating terms and repayment schedules. At what point does the value of their investment in you become uncomfortable for you? And for the sake of really experiencing your comfort zone, imagine **doubling** that amount.

2.   You have the possibility of taking a quantum leap in your career position and salary, or you have the opportunity to go into a new occupation or job altogether [you decide which]. At what point does the value of your new annual income begin to feel uncomfortable or excessive? And for the sake of really experiencing your comfort zone, imagine **doubling** that amount.

Holding onto Abundance

3.   You have been invited to write an article for a magazine, to make a speech to a professional organisation or to perform artistically for an interested group [you decide which]. What is the minimum time you need to comfortably prepare? Now feel what it would be like to cut the preparation time by 50%... or 75%... or 90%... or more... What would it really feel like if you had insufficient time to prepare properly? What if you had to do it *right now?*

4.   You long to go to personal growth seminars, to attend educational classes or to commit to something that increases your health and wellbeing. On your current income, how much money are you prepared to invest in yourself? At what point does it become uncomfortable? And for the sake of really experiencing your comfort zone, imagine **doubling** that amount.

5.   You have made a commitment to work out regularly early each morning at the gym. It's week three, and your alarm clock goes off at its regular time of 5:30AM... 6:00AM [you set the time]. You

know that working out is the healthy choice but you are tired and you know you have an enormous workload facing you that day. How does it really feel to contemplate getting out of bed and going to the gym? How would it feel to contemplate doing this **every** day for the foreseeable future?

Letting Abundance Go

6.   A close friend or family member asks you for an interest-free loan for somewhere between one and five years [you set the period]. It's for a good reason and is important to them. At what point does the amount of the loan start to feel uncomfortable? And for the sake of really experiencing your comfort zone, imagine **doubling** that amount.

7.   You hear rumours that people are going to be laid off at your place of work. You know you have been underperforming, not giving your best of late. Instead you have been keeping your head down and hoping to go unnoticed by your supervisors. You get a phone call from a secretary telling you that you have been summoned to an important meeting with your manager in 15 minutes. How does this **really** feel?

Manifesting Abundance

	A	B	C	D	E
	How did it make you feel to step outside your comfort zone?	What would you have to believe in order to feel this way?	What kind of person feels this way? What does this mean about you?	What will others think about you?	What does this mean about life? Whose beliefs are they anyway?
1					
2					
3					
4					

Holding Onto Abundance

	A	B	C	D	E
	How did it make you feel to step outside your comfort zone?	What would you have to believe in order to feel this way?	What kind of person feels this way? What does this mean about you?	What will others think about you?	What does this mean about life? Whose beliefs are they anyway?
1					
2					
3					
4					

Letting Abundance Go

	A	B	C	D	E
	How did it make you feel to step outside your comfort zone?	What would you have to believe in order to feel this way?	What kind of person feels this way? What does this mean about you?	What will others think about you?	What does this mean about life? Whose beliefs are they anyway?
1					
2					
3					
4					

169

Stage 2

Manifesting Abundance Worksheet

Worksheet For: (Name)

Emotion	Where in Body		What Source says to each level on way back up
→		←	At every level ask 'Are there any specific people related to this feeling?' As soon as someone appears, mark an asterix (*) at that level and STOP ASKING THIS QUESTION. You have now established the Campfire Level
→		←	
→		←	
→		←	
→		←	
→		←	
→		←	
→		←	

Source _____

Stage 3

The Abundance Journey Process

Start with any intense comfort zone / emotional response / fear

Read slowly and carefully. Whenever you see "..." pause and give your partner sufficient time to fully experience the pure, open emotion. Once they have experienced it fully, move on. Start by asking what your partner's strongest emotional issue is. [Write on the Abundance Journey Worksheets] Keep repeating these words going down through the layers until they open into source.

1.   [Say:]

Bring all of your awareness to the feeling

Where in your body is it strongest?

Just allow all the feeling to come flooding... Really welcome it... As you let the feeling grow stronger... ask yourself... What's beneath this?... What's in the core of it?... and feel yourself relaxing and opening right into it...

Just open and drop through to whatever is beneath...

(It may not be at all what you are expecting, so just stay open)...

So, what are you feeling?... [Make sure they name the feeling]

> **At every level until someone shows up ask: "Are there are any specific people related to this feeling?"** Put an asterix (*) at the level that the person appeared, and note who was there. **Once they have named a person, stop asking this question** – you have now established the level of the **campfire**. Keep dropping into source.

Once in source:

> **Source** may be called one of many names, but will be boundary-free, and will have a vast quality such as: freedom; silence; infinite peace; eternal/eternity; God; pure/unconditional love; boundlessness; all that is; consciousness; pure being; awareness; emptiness; cosmos; universe/universal; vastness, etc. Just rest here for a few seconds … and then start washing up through the layers with the words below: repeating them, bringing source up through each level right through the campfire level.

[Now Say:]

Knowing yourself as this vast boundlessness, this stillness, this pure love, this _____ [source], if _____ [source] had something to say to ____ [last level], what would it say? [Let answer.]

[Then Say:] Just allow _____ [source] to wash through _____ [last level.]

> Wash through the Campfire level and then go to the Campfire [the level at which you marked an asterisk].

Campfire Process

[Now Say:]

Imagine a campfire... the nature of which is vast boundlessness, unconditional love and absolute abundance. Imagine a **younger you** sitting at this fire... Now picture the **present you** sitting at the fire... Also at this fire is a **mentor** whose wisdom you trust – it can be someone you know or would like to know, a saint, a sage, or someone born of your imagination, someone in whose divine presence you feel safe, and whose views on abundance are expansive and wise... Now bring to the fire the specific people who are involved with your issue... Regarding any limiting memories or beliefs around abundance, who else should be at this campfire?... [Let answer.]

Can you see the campfire?... Can you see the **younger you?**... The **present you**?... The **mentor**?... Who else is there?... [Let answer. Write down names so you can refer to them specifically, i.e. mother, father, loved one, etc.] Of the people involved with your issue, to which **one or two** would you like to speak?... To whom would you like to speak first?

> Go through **all** points (1 to 13) for **each** person spoken to.

1.　Everyone is now sitting in the protective presence of this fire of unconditional love, acceptance and abundance. The **younger you** may have experienced a great deal of pain in the past around the issue of wealth and abundance. Let the **younger you** speak now from that previous pain, saying what **really** needs to be said, and letting _____ [other person] hear what **really** needs to be heard. [Let answer.]

2.　Knowing that_____ was probably doing the best he/she could with the resources he/she had at the time, let him/her reply. [Let answer.]

3.   Does the **younger you** have anything to reply to that?... [Let answer fully.]

4.   If _____ [other person] were to reply, not from the level of the personality, but from a deeper place, what might he/she say? [Let answer.]

5.   Does the **younger you** have anything to reply to that? [Let answer fully and keep emptying out in this way until fully empty. When all are empty, continue.]

6.   Does the **mentor** have anything to add? [Let answer.]

7.   What does the **present you** have to say to _____? [Let answer fully.]

8.   What would _____ reply from a deeper level? [Let answer fully.]

9.   Does anyone have anything more to add? [Let answer fully. Keep emptying out in this way until empty and continue on to change memory process.]

Change Memory Process

10.   Now allow memories to arise in your awareness – incidents and specific times when you have felt shut down in some way to abundance or wealth in general. What comes up for you? Welcome those times when you have felt diminished or put a lid over abundance in your life. Perhaps there are times when you felt closed off or unable to receive abundance. What specifically took place?

> Be positive and encouraging. Get partner to describe each memory fully and you write down a **brief** description for each specific memory and encourage them to put it up onto a video screen. Then continue.

Now, as you sit peacefully at this fire, let the **younger you** from the memories on the video screen come down from the screen and join you at the campfire... Now ask yourself or your **mentor** what kind of internal emotional resources you COULD have used which would have been helpful at that time...

> Give time to think and come up with resourceful states. Be encouraging and suggest empowering qualities.

Now go ahead and put these resources into a balloon bouquet and hand them to the **younger you**, letting the **younger you** breathe in these qualities, letting them suffuse the whole body. Now let the **younger you** step back onto the video screen, right into the memories, and see and experience them the way they WOULD have happened if you'd had access to these resources at that time... [Long pause.]

So what happened this time ... how was it different? [Let answer.]

> Use the same balloons for each memory, playing them individually anew, from this empowered consciousness.

Now let the **younger you** step down from the screen and rejoin you at the campfire.

Belief Elicitation and Sweep-clean

11.   Now ask yourself, if there were some unhealthy beliefs on abundance that you picked up along the way, what might they be? Sometimes we absorb disempowering beliefs, ideas, and concepts through people's actions, words, societies' conditioning or through our own experience. If there were any remaining unhealthy views on abundance, what might they be? [Let answer fully.]

> Write down each disempowering belief separately.
>
> Continue asking, "What else?", until all beliefs have been elicited.

And now, just ask the mentor to sweep the body of the younger you completely clean and clear of these old limiting beliefs and lies, and any other unhealthy beliefs on abundance that may be present. Let the mentor sweep them out, wash them out, vacuum them out… whichever is appropriate… Just experience how it feels as a complete spring-cleaning of those old issues takes place… And make sure the mentor gets into all the dark corners and hidden or secret places… cleaning everything out at a cellular level… and even deeper, at the level of consciousness… And when this feels complete you can let me know… [Give time.] Great!

Now, if the mentor were to speak from the consciousness of universal abundance, what supportive, empowering and integrative truths would he/she suggest?…

> Read old and then elicit new and empowering truths as antidotes.
>
> Give time. Let answer. Ask mentor for help as appropriate.

Great!... So just allow the **mentor** to install these new, healthy truths into every cell of the body... Just experience how it feels as the **mentor** infuses every fibre of your being with these brand new, wholesome truths... drenching, filling, renewing all of consciousness with positivity and health... And when this is complete you can let me know [Give sufficient time.]... Fabulous! Thank you.

Final Forgiveness

12.   Now, having experienced such a deep sweep-clean, a clear out on all levels, and having learned what you have learned, ask the **younger you** at the campfire, "Even though the other person at the campfire might have had beliefs that were very disempowering, and even though their previous behaviour may not have been acceptable by any standards, and even if you in no way condone their behaviour or beliefs, are you willing **to completely and utterly** forgive them?"... Now go ahead and forgive them from the bottom of your heart. [Let speak forgiveness out loud.]

13.   When the **present you** is ready, ask, "Even though their previous behaviour may not have been acceptable by **any** standards, and even if you in no way condone their behaviour or beliefs, are you willing to **completely and utterly** forgive them from the bottom of your heart?"... Now go ahead and forgive them... [Let speak forgiveness out loud.] You can even make a prayer that somehow they will find self-forgiveness.

[Then say:] Go ahead and forgive all those at the campfire, sending them blessings. Allow them to merge into the light, which is the infinite source of all life. Then turn to the **younger you** and say, "I promise you will never have to experience this again. I forgive you for any pain that was caused, and for not having access to these truths on manifesting and living in abundance at that time, but you can always have access to them any time now. I love you and will always protect you."... Then hugging the **younger you**, let yourself merge, allowing the younger you to grow up with this forgiveness and all these internal resources inside... Turning to the **mentor**, thank him/her... Let the campfire disappear, come back to the present and we will continue going up through the remaining levels. Allow your own awareness to expand spaciously in front, vastly behind and openly to all sides, soaking as an ocean of presence.

[At **each** remaining level, say:] Knowing yourself as this vast boundlessness, this stillness, this pure love, this _____ [source], if _____ [source] had something to say to _____ [last level], what would it say?... [Let answer.]

Just allow _____ [source] to wash over _____ [last level]

> **When all levels are completed, including the top level, read Future Integration at a moderate pace. There is no need to write anything down during the Future Integration.**

Future Integration

[Say:] Having learned what you've learned, having experienced what you've experienced – open into the consciousness of you a day from now, feel how you are feeling, breathe how you are breathing … What do you feel like?... Knowing that you are _____ [source], imagine a situation arising that would have triggered your old issue around abundance. What does _____ [source] say to it?... See how you are handling it healthily now... What kind of things are you doing?... Saying?... Feeling?... How do you feel about yourself?...

Now see yourself a week from now, open into the expanded consciousness, feel how you are feeling, breathe how you are breathing, how are you feeling? Imagine some old abundance issue appearing … What does _____ [source] say to it?... How are you handling it?... What do you look like?... What kind of things are you saying to yourself?... What kinds of healthy actions are you taking?... What are you feeling?...

Step into the future a month from now, open into the consciousness of that time, and feel how you are feeling, breathe how you are breathing. How are you feeling? What if that old situation were to arise?... How are you handling it? What does _____ [source] say to it?... Are you feeling free, confident and light?... What are you saying to yourself?... What are you doing?... How does your body feel?... How are you feeling about abundance in general, about living in abundance on *all* levels?...

Now open into the consciousness of you six months down the line. How are you feeling, about yourself, about abundance in general?...

Now step into the future a year from now, breathe how you are breathing and feel how you are feeling ... What do you feel like?... Are any of the old issues arising or are you feeling free and healthy regarding abundance? If the old issue were to arise, is handling it a breeze now?...

Now step into the future five years from now... open into the consciousness of you five years from now. Feel how you are feeling. How does your body feel?... How are you feeling about abundance?... How are you feeling about living your full potential *as* abundance?...

Now open into the consciousness of you ten years down the road... How are you feeling? ... Breathing? ... Are you feeling so free from these old patterns that they don't even arise anymore? How are you handling things?... How do you feel about yourself and your life?... How do you feel about manifesting abundance?... Holding onto and growing it?... And gracefully letting it flow through you?...

Now, staying connected to the abundance consciousness of the **future you, to the source of you ten years from now** – breathing that way... feeling that way... your cells vibrating at that enhanced level... just ask the **future you** to give some advice to the **present you**, answering the abundance questions from your **new freer, wiser, more wholesome perspective...**

Now repeat two of the scenarios, only this time have your partner experience them from the new abundance consciousness with expanded comfort zones. Then hand the pen and papers to your partner, who will now revisit the remaining elicitation scenarios, discover the new answers to the questions about them (A to E), and write these in the appropriate boxes on the new answer sheets.

[Then say:] In a moment you may open your eyes slowly, staying connected to the future you. And you will find that you will only be able to open your eyes only as soon as all parts of you are fully integrated and have agreed to continue this healing and expansion automatically, perfectly and effortlessly of its own accord, without you having to do or think a thing.

And now, staying wide open in the consciousness of the future you, you may open your eyes when you are ready and revisit the remaining questions from this new truth, from the abundance consciousness of the future you. Let the free, wise future you guide you now!...

Congratulations! Great job!

Let partner answer the remaining questions from the perspective of abundance and freedom, writing their own answers on their new answer sheets.

Stage 4

Effortlessly Attracting Abundance

	A	B	C	D	E
	How did it make you feel to expand your comfort zone?	What would you have to believe in order to feel this way?	What kind of person feels this way? What does this mean about you?	What will others think about you?	What does this mean about life? Whose beliefs are they anyway?
1					
2					
3					
4					

Flourishing and Growing Abundance

	A	B	C	D	E
	How did it make you feel to expand your comfort zone?	What would you have to believe in order to feel this way?	What kind of person feels this way? What does this mean about you?	What will others think about you?	What does this mean about life? Whose beliefs are they anyway?
1					
2					
3					
4					

182

Letting Abundance Graciously Flow

	A How did it make you feel to expand your comfort zone?	B What would you have to believe in order to feel this way?	C What kind of person feels this way? What does this mean about you?	D What will others think about you?	E What does this mean about life? Whose beliefs are they anyway?
1					
2					
3					
4					

183

How to continue your journey:

Support and Information

Our Vision

It is our deep prayer, our passionate mission, to bring these powerfully liberating teachings, these radically transforming tools to people from all backgrounds and walks of life, to countries all across the globe, so that all may realise their deepest human and divine potential and be part of the shift in consciousness our planet needs to heal and flourish.

We pray that every soul has access to this life-changing work and fully awakens to their own abundant potential, and that each of us finds lasting fulfilment in all areas of our life. In uncovering the greatness within, we pray that all of us will be compelled to respond to the global imperative that we be the transformation our planet currently needs, and that together we join the wave of awakening and healing sweeping our world — serving our loved ones, our communities and life itself in bringing consciousness and healing to humanity.

May we all be a living expression of our own deepest abundant potential, our actions be ones of compassion and grace. As beacons of possibility, may we help one another to take our lampshades off, to realise unbridled abundance, and to flourish in abundance-consciousness.

www.thejourney.com

Manifesting
Conscious

Manifest healthy abundance in every area of your life!

The Journey's Manifesting Conscious Abundance programme consists of two radically life-transforming seminars that will forever change your life and have you manifesting your heart's deepest desires in a healthy, conscious way. These programmes will liberate your fullest innate potential and empower you to create conscious, wholesome abundance in every aspect of your life; financial, relationships, health and wellness, creativity - even in these times of global challenge.

Step 1:
The Journey Intensive: laying the foundation

At this dynamic 2-day seminar you'll learn and experience firsthand The Journey's highly-effective tools, which get to the root cause of longstanding issues and clear them completely, creating both emotional and physical healing. This work gives people practical, user-friendly tools to undergo radical transformation and awaken to the true potential inside. Old cell memories and limiting patterns are uncovered, resolved and cleared completely. Emotional blocks that may have held you back for years are eradicated.

The Journey Intensive is a powerful way to face any challenge, clear out any old pattern and step into a new awareness - a new consciousness is the profound gift of this seminar!

Abundance

Live a fulfilling, graceful, joyous life in conscious abundance!

Step 2:
The Manifest Abundance Retreat

This is a powerful 2½-day retreat where you'll meet and uncover your deepest fears, insecurities, negative beliefs and denials - all the ways in which we have created unconscious and destructive behaviours and shut-downs in our lives. With powerful and effective process work you'll expose and liberate all the lies, the 'silent saboteurs', that have kept you small and put a lid on life. In a massive and comprehensive sweep clean, you'll set yourself free from any limitations, negative constructs and blocks, and open into the innate genius inside, which is whole, free and bursting with creative inspiration and solutions. From this vast field of all possibility you'll discover your heart's deepest desires and vision quest your 'brand new' life. You'll leave soaring in your true potential, manifesting a life of greatness, creativity, innovation, love and freedom.

Open into inspired and creative solutions and realise healthy abundance in all areas of your life! Be a proactive force for positive change and act in concert with a higher purpose.

This is your chance to directly experience - to become - a living expression of the greatness that has always been your destiny. This is the wake up call you've been waiting for your whole life. It is time to begin living FULLY in conscious abundance in ALL areas of your life.

The Journey Accredited® Practitioner Programme is possibly the most comprehensive, transformational, in-depth, healing programme available in our time.

It guides and empowers you with a vast array of cutting-edge skills and liberating process work which will powerfully and positively transform every area of your life, allowing your full potential to flourish, freeing you to live life to its fullest. It then enables you to bring that healing transformation and awakening to others, facilitating unbridled freedom and vibrant health.

You'll experience the depth and power of Journeywork at the foundational course, The Journey Intensive. You'll learn that Brandon Bays teaches experientially. She knows that only through experiencing the potency of transformation personally can the true power of the work become part of you.

So imagine what it would be like to absorb through your own direct experience the most profoundly healing therapeutic work available anywhere in the world. Just imagine how powerful that transformation will feel - how liberating and freeing it will be for your spiritual and personal growth. Then imagine how it will feel to powerfully impact and transform the lives of those around you – your loved ones, clients, your community.

How will it feel to be part of the huge wave of awakening and transformation sweeping our planet right now – making a positive contribution to world consciousness with this radical new paradigm for cellular healing and liberation?

As you free yourself, bringing joy, wholeness and peace into every area of your life, you become a living transmission of freedom, which is an embrace that supports others in liberating themselves. You *become* the work. Your very presence becomes a healing, transforming catalyst for change.

> *"Imagine being an integral part of the most profound healing work available in the world today, and being a catalyst for the transformation we'd all love to see for our planet"*

While undergoing this work you will learn cutting-edge skills for getting in deep rapport with your clients. You will learn to open so deeply that those you work with will be carried into that depth. You will experience directly countless individual and in-depth tools, process work and skills that will enable you to work elegantly, precisely, incisively and intuitively with all who are touched by you.

Through the seven courses you will move from student to master of this work and your life will become a living expression of freedom and grace. Ultimately, grace will infuse every aspect of your existence.

Through the course of these seven powerful seminars it will be as if your being is on a jet plane in enlightenment, your essence will become an inspiring, transforming presence that will ignite the fire of awakening in others, catalysing them to begin their healing journeys. You will become a force for positive change in the world - ultimately you will BE the change you wish to see in the world.

The JOURNEY.
Practitioner Programme

SEVEN courses that will forever transform your life

Following The Journey Intensive (described as Step 1 – laying the foundation) you will undergo seven powerfully liberating and healing seminars and retreats.

The Advanced Skills Workshop

An inspiring 1-day seminar, jam-packed with countless powerful tools, process work and skills, which will leave you confident and inspired, ready to begin Journeywork with anyone in your life.

The Manifest Abundance Retreat

At this $2^1/_2$-day residential retreat, you'll forever clear the silent saboteurs that have limited you, exposing and freeing your full potential to effortlessly manifest abundance in all areas of your life. Be part of the co-creative dance of manifestation living in joyous abundance. Includes three nights shared accommodation in a beautiful countryside retreat, all meals, yoga instruction and course materials.

Liberating Kids' Shining Potential Workshop

One fun-filled, joyous, skill-packed day where you learn to be a kid again as you experience simple, exciting, yet powerful work to liberate kids of all ages.

Healing with Conscious Communication

A $2^1/_2$-day weekend filled with powerful, dynamic process work that will open your heart, transforming your ability to communicate consciously, elegantly, effortlessly from your deepest self, facilitating profound healing and transformation with others. Packed with skills and inspiring process work.

The No Ego Retreat

Spend seven days 'in process' in the blazing fire of Truth, deconstructing the scaffolding of your false identity, your ego, exposing the enlightened freedom of your true self. You'll leave soaring in liberation. Residential: Includes seven nights shared accommodation in a gorgeous countryside retreat, all meals, yoga instruction and course materials.

Trainer Training

Spend $2^1/_2$-days at The Journey Intensive deepening and expanding your skills. Learn potent intervention techniques to facilitate profound breakthroughs with yourself and others.

The Practitioner Training Retreat

Go from student to master, from beginner to magician, as you dive into the in-depth work and become a living expression of grace, catalyzing healing on every level with everyone you touch. Residential: Includes eight nights shared accommodation in a beautiful countryside retreat, all meals, yoga instruction and course materials.

The
Visionary Leadership
Programme©

Uncover your own authentic greatness, the innate visionary leader that lies within, and become an agent of conscious transformation in family, career and society.

Join us for the revolutionary new Visionary Leadership Programme© and recognize that you are in fact, already, a leader in business, organizations, sports teams, social groups, and even family and friends. Become an authentic instrument of conscious change.

The Visionary Leadership Foundation:
Uncover your Real Leadership Potential

At The Visionary Leadership Foundation you'll learn effective tools for:

- Clearing out limiting beliefs and social conditioning that stand in the way of true clarity and greatness.

- Dismantling the unconscious behaviours which prevent you from achieving peak performance.

- Learning to deal with emotions - including stress, fear, anxiety - that may have clouded your judgment.

- Uncovering your innate qualities of leadership.

- Becoming an agent for potent personal and professional change.

- You'll leave with more clear-headedness, creativity and energy, a greater freedom of choice, less unhealthy programmed or automatic behaviour, and more calm, focus, simplicity and clarity in your leadership.

Non-Residential: 2-day seminar
Prerequisite: For everyone

"If your actions inspire others to dream more, learn more, do more, and become more, you are a leader."

John Quincy Adams

Visionary Leadership Advanced Retreat 1:
Clear the Hidden Blocks to Your True Leadership Greatness

At Visionary Leadership Advanced Retreat 1 you'll discover how to:

- Identify the qualities you admire most in the world's truly great corporate, political and spiritual leaders and discover how to effortlessly live as an embodiment of those qualities.

- Free yourself from labels, rules and identities that have limited you or kept you small in the past, and open into your fullest potential.

- Uncover and clear the damaging and undermining traps of 'victim', 'defence' and 'blame' games, while taking wholesome responsibility to stand in the truth of your own self.

- Take the 'leadership lampshade' off and let your highest potential radiate as you give unbridled permission and encouragement for others to do the same.

Residential: Includes five nights shared accommodation, meals and course materials.
Prerequisite: The Visionary Leadership Foundation or The Journey Intensive

www.consciouscompany.org

Visionary Leadership Advanced Retreat 2:
Develop Your Leadership Depth, Passion and Vision

At Visionary Leadership Advanced Retreat 2 you'll discover how to:

- Move beyond old paradigms of 'winner-takes-all' competition and harness the exponential power of cooperative competition.

- Uncover and clear specific deep-seated 'ego traps' that have sabotaged and sidelined you in the past and free yourself to operate from an unshakable sense of purpose.

- Free yourself from fears of your physical mortality and unleash a vital energy that will guide and empower you.

- Discover how and why some of your prized values can actually be traps; get clear on which are your true core values, and let them truly support and nurture you.

- Communicate naturally, openly and powerfully to impact and emotionally move others - and enlist their wholehearted cooperation and support.

Residential: Includes five nights shared accommodation, meals and course materials.
Prerequisite: Visionary Leadership Advanced Retreat 1

Visionary Leadership Advanced Retreat 3:
How to Communicate, Present and Live Fully from Authentic Leadership

At Visionary Leadership Advanced Retreat 3 you'll discover how to:

- Elegantly employ the four foundations of conscious presentations
- Speak authentically in public with ease and confidence
- Win and develop deep rapport with your audience
- Present to a group naturally and effectively, from the heart
- Impact your audience, emotionally move them and call them to action
- Work deeply and interactively with an individual while holding the attention of your group
- Communicate from the deepest truth – from pure, mind-free awareness
- Employ guided introspections with groups
- Leave your audience wowed and wanting more…

Residential: Includes five nights shared accommodation, meals and course materials.
Prerequisite: Visionary Leadership Advanced Retreat 2

Other Books by
BRANDON BAYS

The Journey Book

In this paradigm-breaking first book follow Brandon's very personal and remarkable story of healing from a tumour from which she was pronounced textbook perfect after only 6½ weeks, with no drugs or surgery. The profound original process of self-healing, pioneered by her and shared within the pages of this book have since helped hundreds of thousands of people throughout the globe free themselves from lifelong emotional and physical issues.

ISBN: 978-0-7223-3839-5 • Published by: Harper Element

Freedom Is - Liberating Your Boundless Potential

This is a book about freedom - freedom in the truest and deepest sense, freedom on all levels of being. In this remarkable ground breaking book, Brandon doesn't just talk about freedom, she gives you a direct living experience of it. Effortlessly, she guides you into the stillness and joy within, gently liberating emotional blocks, lifting away negative self-concepts, releasing past limitations and opening you into the soaring magnificence of your own self.

ISBN: 0-340-92100-5 • Published by: Hodder Mobius

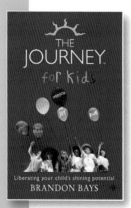

The Journey for Kids - Liberating Your Child's Shining Potential

This book is written from the direct experience of real-life kids' Journeys, and so the children teach us as adults how to partner them in their spiritual and healing journeys. Their stories are so moving, their healing so joyous, their wisdom so simple and true that it's breathtaking. How wonderful it is to be taught the wisdom of the ages through the honest and innocent eyes of a child.

ISBN: 0-00-715526-3 • Published by: Harper Element

www.thejourney.com

JOURNEY
OUTREACH

Journey Outreach

**JOURNEY
OUTREACH**

Also, in addition to Journey Seminars and Visionary Leadership Programmes, both Brandon and Kevin have devoted considerable amount of time and energy to our licensed international charity organisation, Journey Outreach, bringing this healing and transformational work into schools, prisons, addiction and abuse centres, tribal communities, ghettos and aboriginal communities and other places where care giving is brought by people where the need is great and they could not otherwise afford to learn and imbibe these teachings. The work is largely funded by Journey Seminars International and delegates of the work who would like to make a real difference in the world. If you would like to contribute, or to know more about the work, or to make a donation, please contact: www.journeyoutreach.com

This book is an invitation to be part of the wave of awakening our world needs – the choices we make today will affect our own lives, those of our children and grandchildren and they will change the nature of the planet on which humanity lives. If you are inspired by this book in the knowing that consciousness is the only currency that will heal our world, then please pass it on to your friends, your loved ones, your colleagues and everyone who might benefit from this impactful and innovative work. We all deserve to experience true freedom and conscious abundance in our lives.

And, if you would like to know more about Journey and Consciousness Abundance work; if you are ready to roll up your sleeves, meet your deepest fears, clear out any limitations and really dive in to this transformative work, we encourage you to contact our local offices or check our websites. There are seminars taking place all around the world, possibly even close to your home, where you can have a powerful and direct experience of this work. We also encourage you to read the original book, The Journey and to take a look at Brandon Bays' and Kevin Billett's other products and books. Also, there are Journey Practitioners who can guide you through a powerful and personal experience of this work or Conscious Coaches who can offer tailor-made programmes for your businesses and organisations.

Both, Brandon Bays and Kevin Billett offer seminars worldwide throughout the year. If you are interested in experiencing their seminars live, please contact the offices.

UK & EUROPE
PO Box 2, Cowbridge
CF71 7WN, UK
T: +44 (0)1656 890400
infoeurope@thejourney.com

USA & NORTHAMERICA
PO Box 10
Louisville, CO 80027 USA
T: +1 973 680 0271
usainfo@thejourney.com

AUSTRALASIA
PO Box 2015
Byron Bay, NSW 2481, AUS
T: +61 (0) 2 6685 9989
infoaustralia@thejourney.com

AFRICA
PO Box 1870
Bedfordview, 2008, SA
T: +27 11 608 4481
infosa@thejourney.com

www.thejourney.com
www.consciouscompany.org

Additional products by Brandon Bays:

The Journey Book
(Harper Element ISBN 978-0-7223-3839-5)

The Journey Audio Book – read by the author
(Journey Productions ISBN 978-0-9555796-2-2)

The Journey Companion CD – processes from
The Journey book, read by the author
(Journey Productions ISBN 978-0-9555796-1-5)

The Journey for Kids
(Harper Element ISBN 0-00-715526-3)

The Journey for Kids Companion CD – read by the author
(Journey Productions ISBN 978-0-9562017-3-7)

Freedom Is – Liberating Your Boundless Potential
(Hodder Mobius ISBN 0-340-92100-5)

Freedom Is Companion CD
(Journey Productions ISBN 978-0-9555796-4-6)

Power of Vows CD – Satsang with Brandon Bays
(Journey Productions ISBN 978-0-9555796-5-3)

War Zone of The Mind CD
(Journey Productions ISBN 978-0-9555796-6-0)

Meditation CD – led by Brandon Bays
(Journey Productions ISBN 978-0-9555796-3-9)

Additional products by Brandon Bays and Kevin Billett:

Journey Cards
(Journey Productions ISBN 978-0-9555796-0-8)

Healing with Conscious Communication (3 CD Set)
(Journey Productions ISBN 978-0-9562017-9-9)

In Gratitude ...

So many extraordinary people around the world have contributed to Journeywork and Visionary Leadership work, and we couldn't possibly name them all here. But with all our hearts we thank the thousands of beautiful souls whose fierce love of truth and healing brought them to Journey seminars and the Visionary Leadership programmes, to dive in and fully experience the in-depth work. To those who are now offering these tools for transformation and freedom to humanity: you are the real awakeners, the torchbearers, and we all owe you a deep debt of gratitude.

We also thank our core Journey team at our offices around the world. You are models of grace in action. Your surrender to truth and selfless service to humanity take our breath away. We bow to you with all our hearts. One of the greatest blessings of our lives is that we are surrounded by such rare, high quality beings. Everyone who comes to Journey seminars is graced by your devotion, love, and integrity. We will never stop saying thank you for your generous hearts.

From the bottom of our hearts we thank those in the European offices: Gaby, Cliff, Claire, Joanne, Jane, Tricia, Kaye, Paul, Fiona, Michaela, and Stephanie, and our wider team Katrien, Aaron, Ruth and Helena, and our beautiful presenters Debs, Bettina, Arnold, Yvonne and Maarten.

We would like to extend a special thank you to Gaby for your constant daily support, your vision, and for proactively and passionately getting this book to the market; and to Paul for all your detailed research and support in founding Journey Publications. Deep gratitude goes to Joanne for helping to type it all out in Bali, constantly supporting the fine edits and pulling together the content of the book.

In the United States and Canada, huge love and gratitude to Skip, Kristine and their staff, as well as our wonderful presenters Bob and Millie, and the many Journey ambassadors who work so cohesively and beautifully in getting the word out. Thank you all for your passion, dedication, and all your love.

Great love and gratitude to the Australasian team: Phill, Megan, Anné, and Mollie, and to our wonderful presenters Bill, Faizel, Laurie, Tamsyn, Satya, Katrina, Sharon, Tracey-Kim and the many others who support the team.

In South Africa, deep gratitude to Lydia, John, Junior and the extended Journey family that makes it all possible. And huge gratitude to all those who have contributed to Journey Outreach, and particularly those, including the Outreach ambassadors, who actively volunteer their time, energy and love in underprivileged communities around the world, bringing transformation and healing to all they touch. Special thanks to the Journey Outreach board members, who serve selflessly and unconditionally, you are bright beacons and models to us all.

And the worldwide embrace would not be complete without mentioning the amazing Journey Accredited Practitioners, who work with dedication, openness, and love. You are a grace-filled gift to the world. Thank you for your support in making the deeper work available, and thank you for continuing to offer yourself into the fire of liberation.

Thank you all!

Special thanks to all those who have contributed to the formation of Conscious Company and the Visionary Leadership programmes: Campbell, Bill, Skip, Kristine, Claire, Arnold, Bob, Lars, Maarten B, Sree and Lela. And huge thanks to all who have participated in and committed to the work and who so authentically embody its principles of consciousness, truth and selfless service.

A big heartfelt thank you to Catherine Ingram for elegantly editing the first draft of this book with your exquisite and refined touch. And deep gratitude to you for all your wise and enthusiastic support in the formation of our own independent publishing company.

And, most important, we must thank the teachers and masters who have pointed us deeper into freedom, cutting away lies, illusions, and concepts, opening us into this eternal presence. We bow to those teachers, known and not known, whose presence is guiding the huge wave of awakening that is sweeping the globe. There are those who have played immensely powerful roles in our life, and a few must be mentioned here.

Our deep gratitude to Gurumayi, a living experience of enlightenment. Thank you with all our heart Gangaji, for your fierce love and truth speaking, and to the fire of freedom alive in your presence. And to Papaji (Poonjaji), there is no way to fully express our thanks. The heart overflows each moment in gratitude for your grace. Thank you for being such a ruthless fire; for constantly stripping away, consuming all the ideas of who we thought we were; for leaving us no place to land; for forever opening and deepening us in this ocean of love. May every breath be lived as a never-ending prayer of gratitude to your grace. And endless love and gratitude to Ramana Maharshi, who continues to live in our hearts. May your grace continue to liberate thousands of souls.

And finally, profound gratitude to the unseen presence of grace pervading all of life – a grace so benevolent it brought us to the feet of these teachers and continues to consume and liberate everything that is not yet free.

We pray with all of our heart that grace continues to burn through anything and everything that obscures, until there is nothing and no one left — just grace itself. May we all live in the embrace of freedom and grace.